GENOCIDE **&** PERSECUTION

El Salvador and Guatemala

Titles in the Genocide and Persecution Series

GENOCIDE & PERSECUTION

El Salvador and Guatemala

Alexander Cruden
Book Editor

Frank Chalk
Consulting Editor

GREENHAVEN PRESS
A part of Gale, Cengage Learning

GALE
CENGAGE Learning·

Detroit • New York • San Francisco • New Haven, Conn • Waterville, Maine • London

Elizabeth Des Chenes, *Director, Publishing Solutions*

© 2013 Greenhaven Press, a part of Gale, Cengage Learning

Gale and Greenhaven Press are registered trademarks used herein under license.

For more information, contact:
Greenhaven Press
27500 Drake Rd.
Farmington Hills, MI 48331-3535
Or you can visit our Internet site at gale.cengage.com.

For product information and technology assistance, contact us at:

Gale Customer Support, 1-800-877-4253
For permission to use material from this text or product, submit all requests online at www.cengage.com/permissions

Further permissions questions can be emailed to permissionrequest@cengage.com

Every effort is made to ensure that Greenhaven Press accurately reflects the original intent of the authors. Every effort has been made to trace the owners of copyrighted material.

Cover Image Credit: © Andrea Nieto/Getty Images.
Interior barbed wire artwork © f9photos, used under license from Shutterstock.com.

LIBRARY OF CONGRESS CATALOGING-IN-PUBLICATION DATA

El Salvador and Guatemala / Alexander Cruden, Book Editor.
    pages cm. -- (Genocide and persecution)
    Includes bibliographical references and index.
    ISBN 978-0-7377-6254-9 (hardcover)
 1. El Salvador--History--1979-1992. 2. Civil war--El Salvador--History--20th century. 3. Political persecution--El Salvador.--History--20th century. 4. Death squads--El Salvador--History--20th century. 5. State-sponsored terrorism--El Salvador. 6. Guatemala--History--Civil War, 1960-1996--Atrocities. 7. State-sponsored terrorism--Guatemala. 8. Mayas--Crimes against--Guatemala. 9. Genocide--Guatemala. I. Cruden, Alex, editor of compilation. II. Title: El Salvador and Guatemala.
    F1488.3.E344 2013
    972.8405'3--dc23
                                    2012045148

Printed in the United States of America
1 2 3 4 5 6 7 17 16 15 14 13

Contents

Chapter 1: Historical Background on Repression in El Salvador and Guatemala

A UN-directed commission finds that El Salvador's government committed unjustifiable violence and defied international human rights agreements.

Chapter 2: Controversies Surrounding the Repression in El Salvador and Guatemala

A social studies lecturer maintains that the Guatemalan army's strategy evolved from simply killing people it deemed subversive to offering food aid and other protection for those who declared loyalty.

Chapter 3: Personal Narratives

Preface

*"For the dead and the living, we must
    bear witness."*

> Elie Wiesel, Nobel laureate and
> Holocaust survivor

The histories of many nations are shaped by horrific events involving torture, violent repression, and systematic mass killings. The inhumanity of such events is difficult to comprehend, yet understanding why such events take place, what impact they have on society, and how they may be prevented in the future is vitally important. The Genocide and Persecution series provides readers with anthologies of previously published materials on acts of genocide, crimes against humanity, and other instances of extreme persecution, with an emphasis on events taking place in the twentieth and twenty-first centuries. The series offers essential historical background on these significant events in modern world history, presents the issues and controversies surrounding the events, and provides first-person narratives from people whose lives were altered by the events. By providing primary sources, as well as analysis of crucial issues, these volumes help develop critical-thinking skills and support global connections. In addition, the series directly addresses curriculum standards focused on informational text and literary nonfiction and explicitly promotes literacy in history and social studies.

Each Genocide and Persecution volume focuses on genocide, crimes against humanity, or severe persecution. Material from a variety of primary and secondary sources presents a multinational perspective on the event. Articles are carefully edited and introduced to provide context for readers. The series includes volumes on significant and widely studied events like the Holocaust, as well as events that are less often studied, such as the East Pakistan genocide in what is now Bangladesh. Some volumes focus on multiple events endured by a specific people, such as the Kurds, or multiple events enacted over time by a particular oppressor or in a particular location, such as the People's Republic of China.

Each volume is organized into three chapters. The first chapter provides readers with general background information and uses primary sources such as testimony from tribunals or international courts, documents or speeches from world leaders, and legislative text. The second chapter presents multinational perspectives on issues and controversies and addresses current implications or long-lasting effects of the event. Viewpoints explore such topics as root causes; outside interventions, if any; the impact on the targeted group and the region; and the contentious issues that arose in the aftermath. The third chapter presents first-person narratives from affected people, including survivors, family members of victims, perpetrators, officials, aid workers, and other witnesses.

In addition, numerous features are included in each volume of Genocide and Persecution:

- An annotated **table of contents** provides a brief summary of each essay in the volume.
- A **foreword** gives important background information on the recognition, definition, and study of genocide in recent history and examines current efforts focused on the prevention of future atrocities.
- A **chronology** offers important dates leading up to, during, and following the event.
- **Primary sources**—including historical newspaper accounts, testimony, and personal narratives—are among the varied selections in the anthology.
- **Illustrations**—including a world map, photographs, charts, graphs, statistics, and tables—are closely tied

to the text and chosen to help readers understand key points or concepts.

- **Sidebars**—including biographies of key figures and overviews of earlier or related historical events—offer additional content.
- **Pedagogical features**—including analytical exercises, writing prompts, and group activities—introduce each chapter and help reinforce the material. These features promote proficiency in writing, speaking, and listening skills and literacy in history and social studies.
- A **glossary** defines key terms, as needed.
- An annotated list of international **organizations to contact** presents sources of additional information on the volume topic.
- A **list of primary source documents** provides an annotated list of reports, treaties, resolutions, and judicial decisions related to the volume topic.
- A **for further research** section offers a bibliography of books, periodical articles, and Internet sources and an annotated section of other items such as films and websites.
- A comprehensive subject **index** provides access to key people, places, events, and subjects cited in the text.

The Genocide and Persecution series illuminates atrocities that cannot and should not be forgotten. By delving deeply into these events from a variety of perspectives, students and other readers are provided with the information they need to think critically about the past and its implications for the future.

Foreword

The term *genocide* often appears in news stories and other literature. It is not widely known, however, that the core meaning of the term comes from a legal definition, and the concept became part of international criminal law only in 1951 when the United Nations Convention on the Prevention and Punishment of the Crime of Genocide came into force. The word *genocide* appeared in print for the first time in 1944 when Raphael Lemkin, a Polish Jewish refugee from Adolf Hitler's World War II invasion of Eastern Europe, invented the term and explored its meaning in his pioneering book *Axis Rule in Occupied Europe.*

Humanity's Recognition of Genocide and Persecution

Lemkin understood that throughout the history of the human race there have always been leaders who thought they could solve their problems not only through victory in war, but also by destroying entire national, ethnic, racial, or religious groups. Such annihilations of entire groups, in Lemkin's view, deprive the world of the very cultural diversity and richness in languages, traditions, values, and practices that distinguish the human race from all other life on earth. Genocide is not only unjust, it threatens the very existence and progress of human civilization, in Lemkin's eyes.

Looking to the past, Lemkin understood that the prevailing coarseness and brutality of earlier human societies and the lower value placed on human life obscured the existence of genocide. Sacrifice and exploitation, as well as torture and public execution, had been common at different times in history. Looking toward a more humane future, Lemkin asserted the need to punish— and when possible prevent—a crime for which there had been no name until he invented it.

Legal Definitions of Genocide

On December 9, 1948, the United Nations adopted its Convention on the Prevention and Punishment of the Crime of Genocide (UNGC). Under Article II, genocide

> means any of the following acts committed with intent to destroy, in whole or in part, a national, ethnical, racial or religious group, as such:
>
> (a) Killing members of the group;
> (b) Causing serious bodily or mental harm to members of the group;
> (c) Deliberately inflicting on the group conditions of life calculated to bring about its physical destruction in whole or in part;
> (d) Imposing measures intended to prevent births within the group;
> (e) Forcibly transferring children of the group to another group.

Article III of the convention defines the elements of the crime of genocide, making punishable:

> (a) Genocide;
> (b) Conspiracy to commit genocide;
> (c) Direct and public incitement to commit genocide;
> (d) Attempt to commit genocide;
> (e) Complicity in genocide.

After intense debate, the architects of the convention excluded acts committed with intent to destroy social, political, and economic groups from the definition of genocide. Thus, attempts to destroy whole social classes—the physically and mentally challenged, and homosexuals, for example—are not acts of genocide under the terms of the UNGC. These groups achieved a belated but very significant measure of protection under international criminal law in the Rome Statute of the International Criminal

Court, adopted at a conference on July 17, 1998, and entered into force on July 1, 2002.

The Rome Statute defined a crime against humanity in the following way:

> any of the following acts when committed as part of a widespread and systematic attack directed against any civilian population:
>
> (a) Murder;
>
> (b) Extermination;
>
> (c) Enslavement;
>
> (d) Deportation or forcible transfer of population;
>
> (e) Imprisonment or other severe deprivation of physical liberty in violation of fundamental rules of international law;
>
> (f) Torture;
>
> (g) Rape, sexual slavery, enforced prostitution, forced pregnancy, enforced sterilization, or any other form of sexual violence of comparable gravity;
>
> (h) Persecution against any identifiable group or collectivity on political, racial, national, ethnic, cultural, religious, gender . . . or other grounds that are universally recognized as impermissible under international law, in connection with any act referred to in this paragraph or any crime within the jurisdiction of this Court;
>
> (i) Enforced disappearance of persons;
>
> (j) The crime of apartheid;
>
> (k) Other inhumane acts of a similar character intentionally causing great suffering, or serious injury to body or to mental or physical health.

Although genocide is often ranked as "the crime of crimes," in practice prosecutors find it much easier to convict perpetrators of crimes against humanity rather than genocide under domestic laws. However, while Article I of the UNGC declares that countries adhering to the UNGC recognize genocide as "a crime under international law which they undertake to prevent and to punish," the Rome Statute provides no comparable international mechanism for the prosecution of crimes against humanity. A treaty would help individual countries and international institutions introduce measures to prevent crimes against humanity, as well as open more avenues to the domestic and international prosecution of war criminals.

The Evolving Laws of Genocide

In the aftermath of the serious crimes committed against civilians in the former Yugoslavia since 1991 and the Rwanda genocide of 1994, the United Nations Security Council created special international courts to bring the alleged perpetrators of these events to justice. While the UNGC stands as the standard definition of genocide in law, the new courts contributed significantly to today's nuanced meaning of genocide, crimes against humanity, ethnic cleansing, and serious war crimes in international criminal law.

Also helping to shape contemporary interpretations of such mass atrocity crimes are the special and mixed courts for Sierra Leone, Cambodia, Lebanon, and Iraq, which may be the last of their type in light of the creation of the International Criminal Court (ICC), with its broad jurisdiction over mass atrocity crimes in all countries that adhere to the Rome Statute of the ICC. The Yugoslavia and Rwanda tribunals have already clarified the law of genocide, ruling that rape can be prosecuted as a weapon in committing genocide, evidence of intent can be absent when convicting low-level perpetrators of genocide, and public incitement to commit genocide is a crime even if genocide does not immediately follow the incitement.

Several current controversies about genocide are worth noting and will require more research in the future:

1. Dictators accused of committing genocide or persecution may hold onto power more tightly for fear of becoming

vulnerable to prosecution after they step down. Therefore, do threats of international indictments of these alleged perpetrators actually delay transfers of power to more representative rulers, thereby causing needless suffering?

2. Would the large sum of money spent for international retributive justice be better spent on projects directly benefiting the survivors of genocide and persecution?

3. Can international courts render justice impartially or do they deliver only "victors' justice," that is the application of one set of rules to judge the vanquished and a different and laxer set of rules to judge the victors?

It is important to recognize that the law of genocide is constantly evolving, and scholars searching for the roots and early warning signs of genocide may prefer to use their own definitions of genocide in their work. While the UNGC stands as the standard definition of genocide in law, the debate over its interpretation and application will never end. The ultimate measure of the value of any definition of genocide is its utility for identifying the roots of genocide and preventing future genocides.

Motives for Genocide and Early Warning Signs

When identifying past cases of genocide, many scholars work with some version of the typology of motives published in 1990 by historian Frank Chalk and sociologist Kurt Jonassohn in their book *The History and Sociology of Genocide*. The authors identify the following four motives and acknowledge that they may overlap, or several lesser motives might also drive a perpetrator:

1. To eliminate a real or potential threat, as in Imperial Rome's decision to annihilate Carthage in 146 BC.

2. To spread terror among real or potential enemies, as in Genghis Khan's destruction of city-states and people who rebelled against the Mongols in the thirteenth century.

3. To acquire economic wealth, as in the case of the Massachusetts Puritans' annihilation of the native Pequot people in 1637.
4. To implement a belief, theory, or an ideology, as in the case of Germany's decision under Hitler and the Nazis to destroy completely the Jewish people of Europe from 1941 to 1945.

Although these motives represent differing goals, they share common early warning signs of genocide. A good example of genocide in recent times that could have been prevented through close attention to early warning signs was the genocide of 1994 in-flicted on the people labeled as "Tutsi" in Rwanda. Between 1959 and 1963, the predominantly Hutu political parties in power stig-matized all Tutsi as members of a hostile racial group, violently forcing their leaders and many civilians into exile in neighboring countries through a series of assassinations and massacres. Despite systematic exclusion of Tutsi from service in the military, govern-ment security agencies, and public service, as well as systematic discrimination against them in higher education, hundreds of thousands of Tutsi did remain behind in Rwanda. Government-issued cards identified each Rwandan as Hutu or Tutsi.

A generation later, some Tutsi raised in refugee camps in Uganda and elsewhere joined together, first organizing politi-cally and then militarily, to reclaim a place in their homeland. When the predominantly Tutsi Rwanda Patriotic Front invaded Rwanda from Uganda in October 1990, extremist Hutu politi-cal parties demonized all of Rwanda's Tutsi as traitors, ratcheting up hate propaganda through radio broadcasts on government-run Radio Rwanda and privately owned radio station RTLM. Within the print media, *Kangura* and other publications used vicious cartoons to further demonize Tutsi and to stigmatize any Hutu who dared advocate bringing Tutsi into the government. Massacres of dozens and later hundreds of Tutsi sprang up even as Rwandans prepared to elect a coalition government led by moderate political parties, and as the United Nations dispatched a small international military force led by Canadian general Roméo Dallaire to oversee the elections and political transition. Late in 1992, an international human rights organization's investigating team detected the hate propaganda campaign, verified systematic massacres of Tutsi, and warned the international community that Rwanda had already entered the early stages of genocide, to no avail. On April 6, 1994, Rwanda's genocidal killing accelerated at an alarming pace when someone shot down the airplane flying Rwandan president Juvenal Habyarimana home from peace talks in Arusha, Tanzania.

Hundreds of thousands of Tutsi civilians—including children, women, and the elderly—died horrible deaths because the world ignored the early warning signs of the genocide and refused to act. Prominent among those early warning signs were: 1) systematic, government-decreed discrimination against the Tutsi as members of a supposed racial group; 2) government-issued identity cards labeling every Tutsi as a member of a racial group; 3) hate propaganda casting all Tutsi as subversives and traitors; 4) organized assassinations and massacres targeting Tutsi; and 5) indoctrination of militias and special military units to believe that all Tutsi posed a genocidal threat to the existence of Hutu and would enslave Hutu if they ever again became the rulers of Rwanda.

Genocide Prevention and the Responsibility to Protect

The shock waves emanating from the Rwanda genocide forced world leaders at least to acknowledge in principle that the national sovereignty of offending nations cannot trump the responsibility of those governments to prevent the infliction of mass atrocities on their own people. When governments violate that obligation, the member states of the United Nations have a responsibility to get involved. Such involvement can take the form of, first, offering to help the local government change its ways through technical advice and development aid, and second—if the local government persists in assaulting its own people—initiating armed intervention to protect the civilians at risk. In 2005 the United Nations began to implement the Responsibility to Protect initiative, a framework of principles to guide the international community in preventing mass atrocities.

As in many real-world domains, theory and practice often diverge. Genocide and crimes against humanity are rooted in problems that produce failing states: poverty, poor education, extreme nationalism, lawlessness, dictatorship, and corruption. Implementing the principles of the Responsibility to Protect doctrine burdens intervening state leaders with the necessity of addressing each of those problems over a long period of time. And when those problems prove too intractable and complex to solve easily, the citizens of the intervening nations may lose patience, voting out the leader who initiated the intervention. Arguments based solely on humanitarian principles fail to overcome such concerns. What is needed to persuade political leaders to stop preventable mass atrocities are compelling arguments based on their own national interests.

Preventable mass atrocities threaten the national interests of all states in five specific ways:

1. Mass atrocities create conditions that engender widespread and concrete threats from terrorism, piracy, and other forms of lawlessness on the land and sea;
2. Mass atrocities facilitate the spread of warlordism, whose tentacles block affordable access to vital raw materials produced in the affected country and threaten the prosperity of all nations that depend on the consumption of these resources;
3. Mass atrocities trigger cascades of refugees and internally displaced populations that, combined with climate change and growing international air travel, will accelerate the worldwide incidence of lethal infectious diseases;

4. Mass atrocities spawn single-interest parties and political agendas that drown out more diverse political discourse in the countries where the atrocities take place and in the countries that host large numbers of refugees. Xenophobia and nationalist backlashes are the predictable consequences of government indifference to mass atrocities elsewhere that could have been prevented through early actions;

5. Mass atrocities foster the spread of national and transnational criminal networks trafficking in drugs, women, arms, contraband, and laundered money.

Alerting elected political representatives to the consequences of mass atrocities should be part of every student movement's agenda in the twenty-first century. Adam Smith, the great political economist and author of *The Wealth of Nations*, put it best when he wrote: "It is not from the benevolence of the butcher, the brewer, or the baker that we expect our dinner, but from their regard to their own interest." Self-interest is a powerful engine for good in the marketplace and can be an equally powerful motive and source of inspiration for state action to prevent genocide and mass persecution. In today's new global village, the lives we save may be our own.

Frank Chalk

Frank Chalk, who has a doctorate from the University of Wisconsin-Madison, is a professor of history and director of the Montreal Institute for Genocide and Human Rights Studies at Concordia University in Montreal, Canada. He is coauthor, with Kurt

Jonassohn, of The History and Sociology of Genocide *(1990); coauthor with General Roméo Dallaire, Kyle Matthews, Carla Barqueiro, and Simon Doyle of* Mobilizing the Will to Intervene: Leadership to Prevent Mass Atrocities *(2010); and associate editor of the three-volume Macmillan Reference USA* Encyclopedia of Genocide and Crimes Against Humanity *(2004). Chalk served as president of the International Association of Genocide Scholars from June 1999 to June 2001. His current research focuses on the use of radio and television broadcasting in the incitement and prevention of genocide, and domestic laws on genocide. For more information on genocide and examples of the experiences of people displaced by genocide and other human rights violations, interested readers can consult the websites of the Montreal Institute for Genocide and Human Rights Studies (http://migs.concordia.ca) and the Montreal Life Stories project (www.lifestoriesmontreal.ca).*

World Map

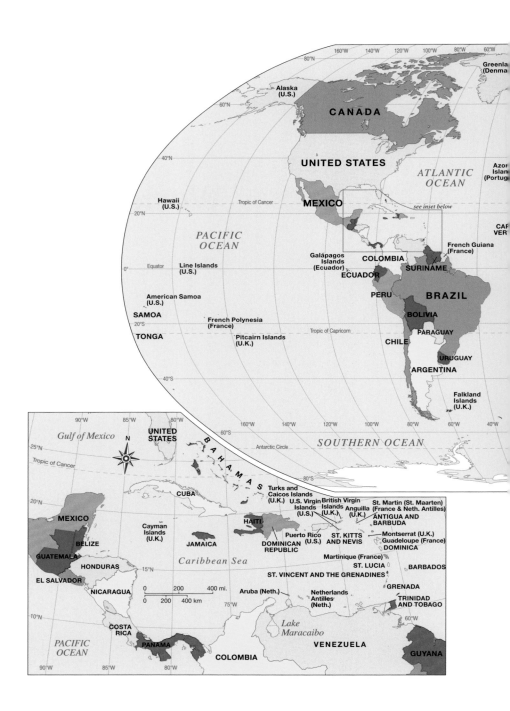

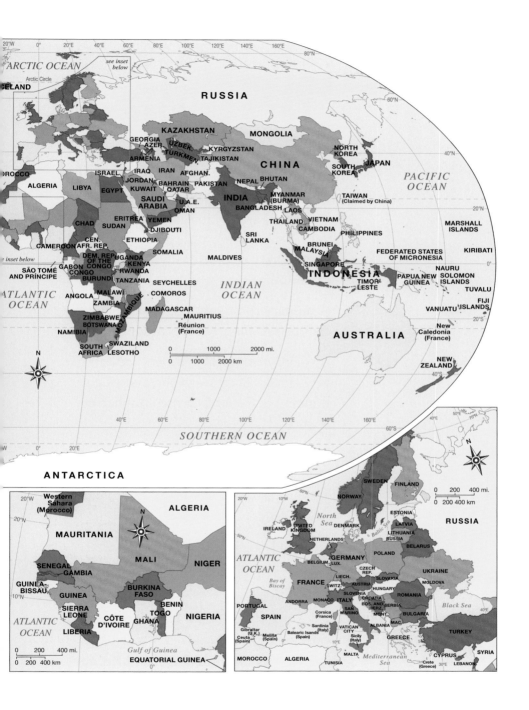

ARCTIC OCEAN

see inset below

Arctic Circle

ICELAND

RUSSIA

KAZAKHSTAN   MONGOLIA

GEORGIA
AZER.   UZBEK.
ARMENIA   TURKMEN.   KYRGYZSTAN
                    TAJIKISTAN

MOROCCO

ISRAEL   IRAQ   IRAN   AFGHAN.

CHINA

NORTH
KOREA

SOUTH
KOREA

JAPAN

PACIFIC
OCEAN

ALGERIA   LIBYA   EGYPT   JORDAN BAHRAIN PAKISTAN
                            KUWAIT QATAR

NEPAL BHUTAN

SAUDI
ARABIA   U.A.E.

INDIA

MYANMAR
(BURMA)

TAIWAN
(Claimed by China)

OMAN

BANGLADESH

LAOS

ERITREA YEMEN

VIETNAM

CHAD

SUDAN   DJIBOUTI

ETHIOPIA

CEN.
AFR. REP.

CAMEROON

SÃO TOME
AND PRÍNCIPE

GABON

DEM. REP.
OF THE
CONGO

CONGO

UGANDA
KENYA
RWANDA
BURUNDI

SOMALIA

THAILAND

CAMBODIA

SRI
LANKA

MALDIVES

PHILIPPINES

BRUNEI

MALAYSIA

SINGAPORE

FEDERATED STATES
OF MICRONESIA

KIRIBATI

MARSHALL
ISLANDS

inset below

TANZANIA   SEYCHELLES

INDONESIA

PAPUA NEW
GUINEA

NAURU   SOLOMON
        ISLANDS

ATLANTIC
OCEAN

ANGOLA

MALAWI

ZAMBIA

COMOROS

INDIAN
OCEAN

TIMOR-
LESTE

TUVALU

VANUATU

FIJI
ISLANDS

ZIMBABWE

BOTSWANA

MOZAMBIQUE

MADAGASCAR

MAURITIUS

AUSTRALIA

New
Caledonia
(France)

NAMIBIA

SOUTH
AFRICA

SWAZILAND

LESOTHO

Réunion
(France)

0   1000   2000 mi.
0 1000 2000 km

NEW
ZEALAND

N

SOUTHERN OCEAN

ANTARCTICA

Western
Sahara
(Morocco)

ALGERIA

MAURITANIA

N

MALI

NIGER

SENEGAL

GAMBIA

GUINEA-
BISSAU

GUINEA

BURKINA
FASO

BENIN

SIERRA
LEONE

CÔTE
D'IVOIRE

TOGO

GHANA

NIGERIA

ATLANTIC
OCEAN

LIBERIA

0   200   400 mi.
0 200 400 km

Gulf of Guinea

EQUATORIAL GUINEA

SWEDEN   FINLAND

NORWAY

0   200   400 mi.
0 200 400 km

North
Sea

ESTONIA

IRELAND   UNITED
KINGDOM

DENMARK

LATVIA

RUSSIA

LITHUANIA

NETHERLANDS

RUSSIA

BELARUS

ATLANTIC
OCEAN

GERMANY

POLAND

BELGIUM LUX.

CZECH
REP.

UKRAINE

Bay of
Biscay

FRANCE

SWITZ.

LIECH.

SLOVAKIA

AUSTRIA   HUNGARY

MOLDOVA

SLOVENIA

ROMANIA

ANDORRA MONACO ITALY

CROATIA

BOS. AND
HERZ.

SERBIA

BULGARIA

Black Sea

PORTUGAL

SPAIN

Corsica
(France)

SAN
MARINO

MONT.

MAC.

VATICAN
CITY

ALBANIA

TURKEY

Gibraltar
(U.K.)

Ceuta
(Spain)

Melilla
(Spain)

Sardinia
(Italy)

Balearic Isands
(Spain)

Sicily
(Italy)

GREECE

CYPRUS

SYRIA

MOROCCO

ALGERIA

TUNISIA

MALTA

Mediterranean
Sea

Crete
(Greece)

LEBANON

17

Chronology

El Salvador

1524–1528   Spanish forces conquer the territory that becomes El Salvador.

1821   El Salvador declares independence from Spain.

1932   Augustin Farabundo Marti leads a peasant rebellion against the government. The military response kills about thirty thousand people.

1961   A military coup puts a right-wing government in charge of El Salvador.

October 15, 1979   A coalition of civilian leaders and military officers overthrows the rightist government of General Carlos Humberto Romero.

November 1979   El Salvador's new government, the Revolutionary Government Junta (JRG), announces several measures to expand democracy.

January 3, 1980   Civilian leaders of the JRG resign after receiving death threats from right-wing elements.

February 6, 1980   US Ambassador Frank Devine says the extreme right in El Salvador is arming itself to help the military against the government and citizens.

February 1980	A former Salvadoran National Guard officer and death-squad commander, Roberto D'Aubuisson, accuses a Christian Democratic Party leader of being a Communist. Days later, that leader is murdered in his home.
March 24, 1980	Archbishop Oscar A. Romero, a religious leader in El Salvador, is assassinated.
March 30, 1980	During the archbishop's funeral, bombs kill forty-two mourners outside the church.
May 7, 1980	D'Aubuisson is arrested along with some of his followers, and the group's weapons are seized in connection with the archbishop's murder. Bowing to right-wing pressure, courts release D'Aubuisson. The military gains more influence in the government.
May 14–15, 1980	Government forces torture and kill hundreds of Salvadoran peasants near the Sumpul River. This begins the civil war that lasts twelve years.
August 12–15, 1980	During a general strike called by a Salvadoran center-left coalition, 129 labor supporters are killed.
October 1980	El Salvador's five largest leftist groups unite in an expansion of the Frente Farabundo Martí para la Liberación Nacional (FMLN).
November 1980	Ronald Reagan wins the presidential election in the United States and says

	he will greatly increase US aid to the Salvadoran military.
November 27, 1980	Seven Salvadoran labor leaders are tortured and murdered.
December 2, 1980	Salvadoran National Guard troops abduct, rape, and murder four US churchwomen: Jean Donovan and nuns Ita Ford, Maura Clarke, and Dorothy Kazel.
December 13, 1980	Installed by the governing junta, José Napoleon Duarte becomes El Salvador's first civilian president in forty-nine years.
January 10, 1981	The FMLN launches attacks on military targets. The military fights back. Hundreds die on both sides.
December 1981	Culminating a year of attacks on Salvadoran peasants, the army kills about one thousand people in the village of El Mozote.
January 1982	Reagan certifies that El Salvador is complying with human rights conditions for receiving US aid.
February– April 1982	Attacking economic targets, the FMLN causes $98 million in damage.
March 17, 1982	Four Dutch journalists are killed in El Salvador.
May–August 1982	The Salvadoran military kills thousands of civilians. President Duarte denounces the killings.
March 16, 1983	Amid the continuing wave of killings, security forces execute the president

of the Human Rights Commission of
El Salvador, Marianela García Villas.

May 25, 1983 Salvadoran rebels fatally shoot a
US military adviser, Colonel Albert
Schaufelberger.

**October–
November 1983** Death squads increase their pace in El
Salvador, killing educators, journal-
ists, labor leaders, and members of the
clergy.

December 9, 1983 US vice president George H.W. Bush
visits El Salvador's capital and says the
death squads must cease because they
threaten the viability of the government.
For a while, killings decrease.

December 1983 FMLN guerrillas plant land mines and
the military responds in force. The result
is an increase in civilian casualties. The
United Nations reports four hundred
thousand Salvadorans are homeless and
another seven hundred thousand have
fled the country—a total of 20 percent of
the population.

May 6, 1984 In a national election, Duarte defeats
D'Aubuisson in a runoff for the presidency.

June 19, 1985 An attack on a restaurant in the
Salvadoran capital kills four US Marines
and nine Salvadoran civilians.

September 1985 The FMLN abducts President Duarte's
daughter, Inés Guadalupe Duarte. A
negotiated settlement exchanges her
and twenty-two mayors for twenty-two

captured rebel leaders. Killings by both sides diminish during the year.

1986–1988	Violence decreases but does not disappear in El Salvador as various parties attempt negotiations. The economy suffers and many people remain homeless.
March 1989	El Salvador elects a right-wing president, Alfredo Cristiani.
April 1989	El Salvador's attorney general is assassinated.
June 1989	Cristiani's chief of staff is assassinated.
November 16, 1989	Salvadoran soldiers kill six Jesuit priests, their housekeeper, and the housekeeper's daughter.
November 11– December 12, 1989	The FMLN launches its largest offensive of the war, attacking military centers throughout the nation. The government responds by bombing cities and killing civilians. The fighting claims two thousand lives on both sides, but the FMLN gains public support.
February 1990	The US House cuts aids to El Salvador in half. The warring sides become more serious about negotiations.
January 2, 1991	Rebels kill three US military advisors near San Miguel, El Salvador.
January 16, 1992	Guided by the United Nations, a peace treaty known as the Chapultepec Peace Agreement ends the civil war in

El Salvador. The cease-fire takes effect February 2, 1992.

November 1992   A UN truth commission begins investigating the civil war.

March 1993   Amnesty is granted in El Salvador for all atrocities during the war.

Guatemala

1523–1524   Defeating indigenous Mayan people, Spanish explorer Pedro de Alvarado declares the area that became Guatemala is now a colony of Spain.

1821   Guatemala declares independence from Spain.

1839   After being a part of regional coalitions, Guatemala becomes fully independent.

1944   Rejecting his repressive predecessors, President Juan Jose Arevalo sets up a social security system, bestows land to landless peasants, and begins other reforms. His election becomes known as the October Revolution.

June 27, 1954   Liberal reforms end as military officer Carlos Castillo takes power in a coup backed by the United States' CIA and the US-based United Fruit Company. For most of the next thirty-plus years, the military rules the country, which becomes known as a banana republic.

1960	A small group of junior military officers splits from the government and begins to help lead an insurgency.
1965	After a series of guerrilla attacks, the Guatemalan army initiates a lethal counter-insurgency, a campaign that becomes genocidal.
1966	US Special Forces join in a Guatemalan army campaign that kills more than eight thousand people.
August 28, 1968	Guerrillas assassinate US Ambassador John Gordon Mein.
1970	Armed forces attack leftists around the country. Over the coming decade at least fifty thousand Guatemalans are killed.
April 5, 1970	Guerrillas assassinate German Ambassador Karl von Spreti.
February 1976	A major earthquake devastates much of Guatemala and corrupt government agencies fail to respond adequately to people's needs in the wake of the disaster.
January 31, 1980	The military attacks the Spanish Embassy, which has been taken over by left-wing activists, and kills thirty-seven people there, including the father of Rigoberta Menchú, who later wins the Nobel Peace Prize in 1992.
1981	With guerrilla resistance mounting, soldiers and unofficial death squads kill tens of thousands of people, wiping out entire villages.

March 23, 1982	Junior army officers stage a coup and ask retired General Efraín Ríos Montt to negotiate a new leadership.
April–June 1982	Ríos Montt declares himself president, voids the constitution, dissolves Congress, and suspends political parties.
July 1982	Ríos Montt tells Guatemalans "If you are with us, we'll feed you; if not, we'll kill you."
1982	The conflict reaches a peak, culminating in the displacement of about one million people.
August 8, 1983	The head of the Defense Department, General Oscar Humberto Mejia Victores, ousts Ríos Montt and declares himself president.
December 2, 1985	Guatemala elects a more moderate president, Vinicio Cerezo of the Christian Democratic Party.
October 1987	Cerezo initiates talks in Madrid, Spain, with Guatemalan guerrilla leaders.
1989	Political violence has continued through the decade, with approximately one hundred thousand killed and forty thousand missing.
January 14, 1991	After a runoff election, the head of a minority party, Jorge Serrano, is inaugurated as president.
May 1993	Serrano, after a failed attempt to fight corruption by restricting civil freedom, flees the country.

1994	Peace talks begin between the government and the Guatemalan National Revolutionary Unity rebels. As negotiations continue, a series of agreements are reached to protect civil rights.
June 23, 1994	A UN-supported Commission for Historical Clarification is created during the peace negotiations. Its mission is to establish the truth of what happened during the conflict.
1995	The United Nations and the United States accuse the Guatemalan government of widespread human rights abuses.
December 1996	Newly elected President Alvaro Arzu ousts senior military officers and signs a peace pact with the rebels.
1998	Human rights activist Bishop Juan Gerardi is murdered.
1999	The Commission for Historical Clarification concludes that security forces were responsible for almost all of the human rights atrocities committed during the last four decades, and that the Guatemalan government committed genocide.
2002	Assassinations, lynchings, and violent crime continue to rise.
July 2006	A Spanish judge, considering atrocities committed over the years in Guatemala, orders the arrest of former leader Ríos Montt and other former officials. Six years later the ex-president is formally indicted.

CHAPTER 1

Historical Background on Repression in El Salvador and Guatemala

Chapter Exercises

STATISTICS

	El Salvador	Guatemala
Total Area	21,041 square km World ranking: 153	108,889 square km World ranking: 107
Population	6.1 million World ranking: 107	14.1 million World ranking: 70
Ethnic Groups	86.3% mestizo (mixed), 12.7% white, 1% Amerindian	59% mestizo (mixed/Ladino) and European, 41% Mayan, <1% other
Religions	57% Catholic, 21% Protestant, 5% other, 17% none	Catholic, Protestant, and indigenous Mayan beliefs (percentages not available)
Literacy (total population)	81%	69%
GDP	$45.98 billion World ranking: 99	$78.42 billion World ranking: 83

Source: *The World Factbook*. Washington, DC: Central Intelligence Agency, 2012. www.cia.gov.

1. Analyzing Statistics

Question 1: Ethnicity plays a role in many genocides; based on the statistics and your knowledge of the events, what role did ethnicity play in the incidents in Guatemala and El Salvador?

Question 2: Based on the statistics above, in which country do people live closer together?

Question 3: Based on the statistics above, in which of the two countries are people poorer, on average?

2. Writing Prompt

Choosing either country as your subject, write an article about how its truth commission investigated what happened and assigned responsibility. Include details and examples of the commission's methods. Then put a strong title on your article that will attract readers.

3. Group Activity

Divide into small groups, with each group analyzing US involvement in one or both of the conflicts covered in Chapter 1. Then each group should present a brief summary of what would have been the best US response in the circumstances.

In El Salvador, a Military and Police Campaign Attacked Civilians

Cynthia J. Arnson

Government repression, election fraud, and an economy ruled by an elite few laid the groundwork for a twelve-year civil war in the small Central American country of El Salvador, a scholar asserts in the following viewpoint. The majority of the war's victims were villagers, farm families, and the urban poor. Tens of thousands of people were massacred during the 1980–1992 conflict by government forces who received US support. Guerrillas fought back with kidnappings and executions. Cynthia J. Arnson is director of the Latin American program of the Woodrow Wilson International Center for Scholars and was previously associate director of Human Rights Watch.

Between 1980 and 1992, the tiny Central American republic of El Salvador was engulfed in a brutal civil war. The Salvadoran armed forces, internal security forces such as the National Guard and National Police, and death squads allied with them killed tens of thousands of Salvadoran civilians in an effort to wipe out the guerrilla insurgency of the Farabundo Martí National Liberation Front (FMLN). Throughout the conflict, but most particularly in

Cynthia J. Arnson, "El Salvador," *Encyclopedia of Genocide and Crimes Against Humanity*, edited by Dinah L. Shelton. Farmington Hills, MI: Macmillan Reference, 2005, pp. 282–286. Copyright © 2005 Cengage Learning. All rights reserved. Reproduced by permission.

its early years, state forces committed grave and systematic abuses of human rights, including massacres, murders, disappearance, and torture. The FMLN carried out a smaller but nonetheless serious number of violations of international humanitarian law, including targeted assassinations of prominent public figures, kidnappings for ransom, and harming civilians in violation of the rule of proportionality of the laws of war. A United Nations-sponsored Commission on the Truth for El Salvador, created in 1992 as part of a UN-brokered peace accord, concluded that 85 percent of the human rights cases brought to its attention involved state agents, paramilitary groups, or death squads allied with official forces. Five percent of cases brought to the Truth Commission were attributed to the FMLN.

Political factors that led to the outbreak of war included decades of military rule, blatant fraud when civilians won the 1972 and 1977 presidential elections, and increasingly violent suppression of the regime's opponents. These political factors were coupled with the domination of the economic life of the country by a small landed elite that was opposed to reforms, especially agrarian reform, and who derived their control from the economic transformation of the country in the late nineteenth century. That period saw the rapid expansion of coffee cultivation, the abolition of indigenous tribal lands, and the creation of rural police forces for the explicit purpose of evicting peasants from communally held properties.

A landmark event in El Salvador's modern history was the 1932 peasant revolt, which was prompted by worldwide depression and plunging coffee prices. In December 1931, Minister of War General Maximiliano Hernández Martínez seized power in a military coup. Poorly armed and poorly organized peasants staged an uprising, led by communist organizer Farabundo Martí (from whom the latter-day guerrillas took their name). In quelling the rebellion, Hernández Martínez and his troops massacred between 10,000 and 30,000 people in a matter of weeks. According to the U.S. Central Intelligence Agency (CIA), in a

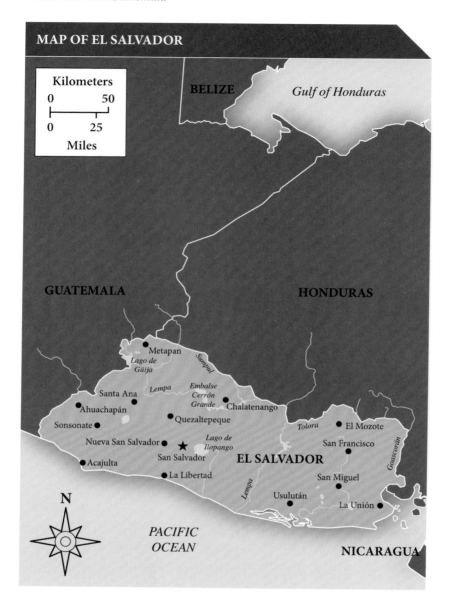

MAP OF EL SALVADOR

Kilometers
0   50
0   25
Miles

BELIZE   *Gulf of Honduras*

GUATEMALA   HONDURAS

Metapan
Lago de Güija
Santa Ana   *Lempa*   *Embalse Cerrón Grande*
Ahuachapán   Chalatenango
Sonsonate   Quezaltepeque
Nueva San Salvador   *Lago de Ilopango*   *Tolora*   El Mozote
Acajulta   San Salvador   San Francisco
La Libertad   **EL SALVADOR**
San Miguel
N   Usulután
La Unión
PACIFIC OCEAN   NICARAGUA

1985 assessment, "the resulting endemic national paranoia over the Communist threat reinforced authoritarian rule by the armed forces and its affluent civilian backers for the next half century. The chain of military regimes provided order and stability, and largely gave the plantation owners and monopolist businessmen a free hand over the economic life of the country."

Political violence dramatically increased in 1979, following a reformist military coup aimed at staving off a violent revolution like the one that had begun in 1978 in neighboring Nicaragua. Efforts by military officers and progressive civilians to promote reforms, including an end to human rights abuses, were blocked by a wave of violence unleashed by the army and security forces. Through mass demonstrations and sit-ins, grassroots organizations, some with direct or indirect links to guerrilla groups that had emerged in the early 1970s, challenged the junta to rapidly fulfill its promises. Targeted killings by state forces and increasing confrontations between government troops and demonstrators brought the civilian death toll to a record 9,000 to 10,000 in 1980. High-profile victims included El Salvador's Archbishop, Oscar Romero, who was shot by a death squad as he celebrated mass. Six leaders of the leftist political opposition were kidnapped by security forces from a press conference and then tortured and murdered, and four U.S. churchwomen were abducted, raped, and killed by troops of the National Guard. Amid the escalating repression, guerrilla groups coalesced to form the Farabundo Martí National Liberation Front (FMLN). Their failed "final offensive" in January 1981 effectively launched the country into full-scale civil war.

US Involvement Is Controversial

The years 1980 to 1983 witnessed the heaviest repression. Massacres in rural areas, gruesome murders by death squads, and the killing or disappearance of teachers, trade unionists, students, religious and humanitarian workers, journalists, and members of opposition political parties were the products of a military mindset that equated opposition with subversion and that viewed civilians in combat zones as legitimate targets of attack. The scale of the killings in rural as well as urban areas subsided in the second half of the decade, largely as the result of pressure from the United States, which provided approximately $6 billion in military and economic assistance to the Salvadoran government over the course of the war. El Salvador became one of the most contentious U.S. foreign policy issues of the cold war. Pressure for improvements in human rights originating in the U.S. Congress was coupled with the persistent downplaying or outright denial of abuses by senior U.S. authorities who were concerned with maintaining a flow of aid to defeat the insurgency.

The December 1981 massacre in El Mozote and surrounding villages epitomized both Salvadoran army practices and the pattern of U.S. denial. According to the Truth Commission, the army's elite Atlacatl Battalion "deliberately and systematically" executed more than 500 men, women, and children over a period of several days, torturing some victims and setting fire to buildings. Exhumations in and around El Mozote after the war revealed that, in one parish house alone, 131 of the 143 victims were children whose average age was six. The Truth Commission found "no evidence" to support arguments made publicly by the U.S. government at the time of the massacre that the victims had participated in combat or had been trapped in crossfire between combatant forces.

Other large-scale massacres of civilians in rural areas took place at the Sumpul River (1980), San Francisco Guajoyo (1980), El Junquillo (1981), the Lempa River (1981), El Calabozo (1982), Las Hojas (1983), the Gualsinga River (1984), Los Llanitos (1984), and San Sebastián (1988). While the death toll in massacres subsided as the decade wore on, hundreds of civilians were killed and many more thousands were displaced or forced to flee the country by indiscriminate aerial bombing campaigns conducted by the Salvadoran Air Force from 1983 to 1986. The goal was to drive civilians out of zones where the guerrillas were active. Bombing attacks subsided after 1986, a result of international pressure and a change in FMLN tactic, which emphasized small unit operations over the massing of large numbers of fighters.

Guerrilla abuses against the civilian population took place mainly but not exclusively in the context of the conflict. Before the outbreak of war, the guerrillas kidnapped prominent individuals for ransom, including the Salvadoran foreign minister in 1978 (he was subsequently executed). Beginning in the 1970s and continuing throughout the conflict, the FMLN summarily executed civilians suspected of being government informants. Such individuals were known as *orejas*, or "ears."

Targeted killings and disappearances of civilians by the FMLN were smaller in number than those of state forces, but constituted serious violations of international humanitarian law, nonetheless. Victims included more than eleven mayors, who were executed between 1985 and 1988 in areas the guerrillas considered their zones of control. Also killed were four off-duty U.S. Marines, who were machine-gunned at an outdoor café in 1985; and conservative public figures such as Attorney General José Roberto García Alvarado and intellectual Francisco Peccorini, both assassinated in 1989. Other episodes of FMLN abuse included the mass execution of a group of captured civilians in Morazán (1984), the kidnapping of the daughter of President José Napoleón Duarte (1985), and the killing of civilians who refused to stop at guerrilla roadblocks. Scores of civilians were killed and hundreds were wounded by the guerrillas' indiscriminate use of land mines. On numerous occasions, the use of crude and inaccurate homemade weapons and explosives resulted in civilian deaths.

Death Squads Spread Terror

Nothing so epitomized the terror of the Salvadoran war as the activities of the death squads. According to the Truth Commission, the squads' share of abuses was relatively small (just over 10% of documented cases), but they "gained such control that they ceased to be an isolated or marginal phenomenon and became an instrument of terror used systematically for the physical elimination of political opponents." The Truth Commission reported

that civilian as well as military authorities during the 1980s participated in, encouraged, and tolerated death squad activities, offering "complete impunity" for those who worked in them.

Official U.S. documents that were declassified after the end of
the war contain a wealth of information on death squad operations,
structure, and personnel. For instance, Roberto D'Aubuisson, a
cashiered National Guard officer, was a key figure in death squad
violence. According to the U.S. Embassy in San Salvador, one of
his most notorious crimes was overseeing the drawing of lots for
the "privilege" of assassinating Archbishop Romero. According to
a 1981 CIA memo, D'Aubuisson was funded by members of the
"extreme right-wing Salvadoran elite" who "have reportedly spent
millions of dollars" in an effort to return the country to right-wing
military rule. Another 1981 CIA report said that D'Aubuisson favored the "physical elimination" of leftists, whom he defined as
"anyone not supportive of the traditional status quo." According
to the Truth Commission, D'Aubuisson maintained close contact
with the intelligence sections of the security forces, combining
"two elements in a strategic relationship": money (and weapons,
vehicles, and safehouses) provided by the extreme right, and ideology, providing "the definition of a political line," for the intelligence units of the security forces.

To give a political front to the death squads, D'Aubuisson
organized the *Frente Amplio Nacional* (Broad National Front),
which later became the Nationalist Republican Alliance (*Alianza
Republicana Nacionalista*, or ARENA) party. As ARENA'S candidate, D'Aubuisson was elected to the Constituent Assembly in
1982, later becoming its president. From that post, according to
the CIA in 1984, he directed a team that engaged in "political intimidation, including abduction, torture, and murder." In 1985,
the CIA identified the notorious Secret Anticommunist Army
(*Ejército Secreto Anticomunista*, or ESA) as the public face of the
ARENA death squad.

Other death squads operated out of the military and security
forces, occasionally conducting joint operations. These included

Photos of those who disappeared during the civil war in El Salvador are displayed in San Salvador on the eve of the Day of the Dead celebration, held every year to commemorate deceased relatives. © Jose Cabezas/AFP/Getty Images.

death squads organized out of the intelligence sections of the National Guard and National Police. The army's First Brigade, Signal Corps, Second Brigade, and cavalry, artillery, engineer, and infantry detachments throughout the country also participated in death-squad killings. A death squad operating out of an intelligence unit of the Air Force in the early 1990s threw bound but living prisoners out of aircraft over the Pacific Ocean, a practice referred to as "night free-fall training."

Negotiations to end the Salvadoran conflict began in late 1989, the result of a military stalemate, the end of the cold war, and the international disrepute of the armed forces following the army's murder of six prominent Jesuit priests. This atrocity led to a human rights case with broad international repercussions. The sweeping accord signed in 1992 under UN auspices established a Truth Commission composed of non-Salvadorans to investigate grave acts of violence, and an Ad Hoc Commission of Salvadoran citizens to review the records of military officers with an eye to purging those who had violated human rights. Those recommended for dismissal eventually included the minister and vice-minister of defense. The accord also abolished the security forces, established a new National Civilian Police, and reduced the role of the military in postwar society. While most of the provisions of the peace accord were implemented, the majority of the recommendations of the Truth Commission remained unfulfilled. In 1993, amid death threats and high-profile killings of demobilized FMLN leaders, the Salvadoran government created a Joint Group (*Grupo Conjunto*) for the Investigation of Politically Motivated Illegal Armed Groups. It found that politically motivated violence was linked to "the broad network of organized crime" operating in El Salvador, and raised questions about the ties between earlier death squad participants and the "highly organized criminal structures" engaged in a host of illegal activities, including drug trafficking.

US Policy Was Inconsistent as Fighting Grew in El Salvador

Richard A. Haggerty

Around 1980, at the time the conflict in El Salvador was erupting into full-scale civil war, US policy toward the country was inconsistent, a US-commissioned report says. In the following viewpoint, the author asserts that, on one hand, US president Jimmy Carter's administration was trying to prevent a left-wing takeover of El Salvador. On the other hand, the Carter administration was trying to protect human rights. But the rights violations, including mass killings, originated with the anti-leftist government. Starting in 1981, the Reagan administration's approach emphasized the anti-communism effort, added economic aid, and encouraged some human-rights efforts favored by the US Congress. Richard A. Haggerty has written three books about Latin American countries.

The [Jimmy] Carter administration had lost considerable leverage in El Salvador when the [Carlos Humberto] Romero [Mena] government renounced United States aid in 1977. The United States therefore welcomed the October 1979 coup and backed up its approval with an economic aid package that by 1980 had become the largest among Western Hemisphere

Richard A. Haggerty, "The United States Takes a Hand," *El Salvador: A Country Study.* Washington, DC: US Government Printing Office, 1988.

recipients. A small amount of military aid also was provided. United States advisers contributed to the third junta's agrarian reform program, particularly Phase III, of the reform, the so-called Land to the Tiller decree of April 28, 1980, granting title to smallholders. Phase II, expropriating holdings between 100 and 500 hectares, was decreed in March 1980, but implementation was postponed. The government cited lack of administrative and financial resources for its inaction; many observers believed that political considerations were equally influential.

United States policy and influence in El Salvador, however, was fitful and inconsistent from 1979 through 1981. It was driven by two conflicting motivations in the complex and shifting political prism of El Salvador. The first motivation was the prevention of a leftist takeover. Both economic and military aid for the junta governments seemed to be intended to promote a centrist alternative to either a Marxist-led revolution or a conservative military regime. The assumption of power by the FSLN [Frente Sandinista de Liberación, a socialist political party] in Nicaragua increased the pressure on the United States to prevent a similar result in El Salvador; this pressure grew by 1981 as the Sandinistas consolidated their dominant role in the Nicaraguan government.

The second motivation was human rights. The Carter administration had established the promotion of human rights as a cornerstone of its foreign policy, particularly in Latin America. Like many Salvadorans, United States officials were frustrated by the inability of the junta governments to contain political violence. Nevertheless, Carter's policy was sufficiently flexible to allow increased aid levels despite a generalized upswing in human rights violations in El Salvador, as long as the government there appeared to be making good faith efforts at reform. It was not merely the general level of violence, however, but the specific murders of United States citizens that most affected dealings with El Salvador. . . . The December 1980 murder of . . . four churchwomen produced a complete cutoff of aid pending

A Firebrand Officer Polarizes His Country

Roberto D'Aubuisson Arrieta (1943–1992) may be the most divisive individual in the history of El Salvador. One US ambassador to the country called him a "pathological killer." Another described him as a "dynamic leader." He was a hero to anti-Communist conservatives and an archvillain to the left wing.

The son of middle-class parents, D'Aubuisson had a military education, including a couple of post-graduate years of US training. He rose in the Salvadoran army and became politically prominent as a hard-line right-winger. Although he did not succeed in being elected president, the party he founded was dominant in the 1980s, and he held several high positions.

D'Aubuisson was thought to be the mastermind of infamous assassinations—including those of six Jesuit priests, the country's attorney general, and Archbishop Oscar Arnulfo Romero—and the godfather of death squads that killed thousands of people. He denied all the accusations and never stood trial. As the civil war came to an end, D'Aubuisson surprisingly turned peacemaker, cautioning the right wing against stopping the negotiations. He died of throat cancer at age forty-eight.

an investigation of the case. On January 4, 1981, two American land reform advisers from the American Institute for Free Labor Development (AIFLD) were gunned down along with a Salvadoran in the Sheraton Hotel in San Salvador. This action alarmed not only the White House but also the United States Congress, and it added fuel to the effort to disburse aid based on improvements in the Salvadoran human rights situation.

The launching of the "final offensive" lent a new urgency to Washington's approach. On January 14, 1981, four days after the offensive began, Carter announced the approval of US$5 million in "nonlethal" military aid; an additional US$5 million

Three nuns kneel near the bodies of nuns kidnapped and killed by the Salvadoran Army in July 1980. The murders of the four American nuns, as well as other killings of US citizens, led the United States to re-examine its relationship with the government of El Salvador. © AP Images/ Valente Cotera.

was authorized four days later. The low level of the aid and the impediments to its rapid disbursement meant that it had little direct impact on the Salvadoran armed forces' response to the guerrilla offensive; the renewal of military aid, however, established a trend that President [Ronald] Reagan would build on when he assumed office on January 20, 1981.

Policy Was Reshaped Under Reagan

The Reagan administration initially appeared to stress the need to shore up El Salvador as a barrier against communist expansion in Central America. The United States Department of State issued a special report on February 23, 1981, entitled *Communist Interference in El Salvador*, which emphasized Nicaraguan, Cuban, and Soviet support for the FMLN [Farabundo Martí National Liberation Front, a guerrilla group]. The report was widely criticized in the American media and the United States Congress. Nevertheless, the administration succeeded in increasing substantially the levels of United States military and economic aid to El Salvador, first by executive order, then by legislative appropriation. Although Reagan downplayed the importance of human rights considerations, Congress voted in January 1982 to require certification by the executive every six months of Salvadoran progress in such areas as the curbing of abuses by the armed forces, the implementation of economic and political reforms (particularly agrarian reform), and the demonstration of a commitment to hold free elections with the participation of all political factions (all those that would renounce further military or paramilitary activity). The administration accepted the certification requirement, albeit reluctantly, and proceeded with a policy that emphasized economic maintenance in the face of guerrilla attacks on the country's infrastructure, military buildup to contain the insurgency, and low-key efforts in the human rights area.

With the War's End, Salvadorans Have a Chance to Rebuild

Michael Reid

In the following viewpoint, a journalist reports on the end of the civil war in El Salvador in early 1992. The truce included a structure for full democracy, cutting the armed forces by half, and land redistribution. However, the author maintains, El Salvador needed US$1.8 billion from other countries to restart its war-shattered economy. Widespread poverty and economic uncertainty, along with fears of renewed death-squad violence, cast serious doubts on how El Salvador could become a thriving democratic nation. Reporter and author Michael Reid is the Americas editor of The Economist.

On Sunday [February 2, 1992] Central America will take another important step away from the violence that enveloped it in the 1980s. An official ceasefire will at last come into effect in El Salvador after 12 years of bloody civil war. According to the agreement signed in Chapultepec Castle in Mexico City this month between President Alfredo Cristiani's rightwing government and the leftwing FMLN [Farabundo Martí National Liberation Front] guerrillas, what should happen next is not just peace but also an experiment unique in Latin America.

Under the supervision of more than 1,000 United Nations observers, an internationally endorsed programme of reform is to be enacted over the next two years that should make El Salvador a recognisable democracy.

The reforms involve a 50 percent cut in the armed forces and their subordination to the civil power, a purge of the more notorious military violators of human rights, a new civilian police force, the creation of fairer electoral and judicial systems and in guerrilla-controlled areas, modest transfers of land to those occupying it. In return, the FMLN is to disarm its 8,000 or so fighters by October 31, and will be allowed to become a legal political party.

This programme of liberal democracy is a long way from the socialist revolution officially espoused by the FMLN until 1984. Nevertheless, it is still opposed by sections of Mr Cristiani's Arena Party, as well as by part of the army.

Mistrust runs deep. Fears are widely held of a return to death squad violence as the hard-right attempts to disrupt the difficult transition to peaceful democracy, intended to culminate in a presidential election in 1994.

It has taken 75,000 dead—most of them civilians—hundreds of thousands of refugees, and almost two years of tense talks to reach this point. What ended at Chapultepec Castle was one of the most durable local conflicts fought against the background of the cold war.

The War Began with Little Global Notice

The world took little notice when the Salvadorean armed forces stole elections from reformers in 1972 and 1977, virtually forcing those who wanted change to take up arms. Then by the time the guerrilla bombings and death-squad massacres had developed into civil war, the Sandinista revolution had triumphed in Nicaragua and the long-standing guerrilla war in Guatemala had intensified. Central America, and El Salvador in particular, was where [US Secretary of State] Alexander Haig said Washington would 'draw the line' against world communism.

A Centrist Tried to Keep Stability During War

José Napoleón Duarte (1925–1990) was president of El Salvador for much of the civil war (1980–1982 and 1984–1989), yet was not a hard-liner. The central struggle of Duarte's public life was between compromising and leading. The way he put it: "My obligation lay in freeing my country from the two totalitarian extremes: the Marxists and the fascists."

Born to an affluent family in the capital, San Salvador, Duarte had an excellent education, culminating with a degree in civil engineering from Notre Dame University in the United States. He turned to politics only later in life, yet rose quickly when he did. He became a leader in the moderate Christian Democratic Party, which grew rapidly in the 1960s in El Salvador and was elected three times as the capital city's mayor.

His first presidency came about only after he agreed to become part of a military junta. Severely criticized from both the Left and the Right and supported intermittently by the United States, Duarte struggled to chart an effective course between large-scale reform and reactionary force. He failed to halt the death squads that massacred civilians, did not achieve his goal of land redistribution, and was unable to negotiate an end to the civil war. Shortly after leaving the presidency, he died of stomach cancer at age sixty-four.

Trapped in this cold-war scenario, El Salvador's conflict became a stalemate of 'low-intensity' attrition. US aid—eventually to total more than $4 billion—and counter-insurgency training stiffened the army enough for it to prevent a guerrilla victory.

It took the FMLN's 1989 offensive, in which the guerrillas held parts of the capital for several days, to convince the newly-elected Mr. Cristiani and his business backers to open serious talks. During the offensive, the army managed to turn a military victory into a self-inflicted political defeat by dragging six Jesuit priests from their beds and murdering them.

But it was not until last September, after the failure of the Moscow coup—and the definitive end of the cold war—that the [George H.W.] Bush administration finally abandoned lingering hopes of a military victory and threw its weight fully behind the peace talks.

The government estimates that it needs $1.8 billion in international aid to reconstruct the war-torn economy. The auguries are not good. Nicaragua and Panama have both found that US aid has been inadequate in relation to the needs of economies battered by war and sanctions. Poverty remains the principal underlying threat to democracy in Central America.

Centre-right civilian governments are now applying laissez-faire economics throughout the isthmus. They are in tune with the Bush administration and its free trading 'initiative for the Americas'. But so far, they have yet to raise the living standards of their peoples.

The FMLN and its supporters say they want to form a broad centre-left reformist coalition—including the Christian Democrats, who under the late José Napoleón Duarte were their foes. But as their counterparts elsewhere in the region have found, the FMLN may end up having to sacrifice economic demands in return for a stable transition to democracy.

The Government of El Salvador Violated International Standards

United Nations

In 1992, the United Nations Security Council created the Commission on the Truth for El Salvador to independently report on the Salvadoran civil war. In the following viewpoint, the UN concludes that the country's government violated the international human rights treaties it signed, and thus its conduct during the war was unjustifiable. Commission members traveled throughout El Salvador and found that while both sides were guilty of killings and other uses of force, the military was far more to blame than the guerrillas and later tried to cover up its atrocities. The truth commission was appointed by the UN secretary-general, and the chairman was the former president of Colombia, Belisario Betancur.

Commission on the Truth was so named because its very purpose and function were to seek, find and publicize the truth about the acts of violence committed by both sides during the war.

The truth, the whole truth and nothing but the truth, as the oath goes. The overall truth and the specific truth, the radiant but quiet truth. The whole and its parts, in other words, the bright light shone onto a surface to illuminate it and the parts of this same surface lit up case by case, regardless of the identity of the perpetrators, always in the search for lessons that would contribute to reconciliation and to abolishing such patterns of behaviour in the new society.

Learning the truth and strengthening and tempering the determination to find it out; putting an end to impunity and cover-up; settling political and social differences by means of agreement instead of violent action: these are the creative consequences of an analytical search for the truth.

Furthermore, by virtue of the scope which the negotiators gave to the agreements, it was understood that the Commission on the Truth would have to examine systematic atrocities both individually and collectively, since the flagrant human rights violations which had shocked Salvadorian society and the international community had been carried out not only by members of the armed forces but also by members of the insurgent forces.

The peace agreements were unambiguous when, in article 2, they defined the mandate and scope of the Commission as follows: "The Commission shall have the task of investigating serious acts of violence that have occurred since 1980 and whose impact on society urgently demands that the public should know the truth", Article 5 of the Chapultepec Peace Agreement [which ended the war] gives the Commission the task of clarifying and putting an end to any indication of impunity on the part of officers of the armed forces and gives this explanation: "acts of this nature, regardless of the sector to which their perpetrators belong, must be the object of exemplary action by the law courts so that the punishment prescribed by law is meted out to those found responsible".

It is clear that the peace negotiators wanted this new peace to be founded, raised and built on the transparency of a knowledge which speaks its name. It is also clear that this truth must be made public as a matter of urgency if it is to be not the servant of impunity but an instrument of the justice that is essential for the synchronized implementation of the agreements which the Commission is meant to facilitate.

The Work Was Long and Arduous

From the outset of their work, which began on 13 July 1992 when they were entrusted with their task by the Secretary-General of the United Nations, the Commissioners could perceive the skill of those who had negotiated the agreements in the breadth of the mandate and authority given to the Commission. They realized that the Secretary-General, upon learning from competent Salvadorian judges of the numerous acts of violence and atrocities of 12 years of war, had not been wrong in seeking to preserve the Commission's credibility by looking beyond considerations of sovereignty and entrusting this task to three scholars from other countries, in contrast to what had been done in Argentina and Chile after the military dictatorships there had ended. The Commissioners also saw a glimmer of hope dawn in the hearts of the Salvadorian people when it became clear that the truth would soon be revealed, not through bias or pressure but in its entirety and with complete impartiality, a fact which helped to restore the faith of people at all levels that justice would be effective and fitting. Accordingly, in their first meeting with the media upon arriving in El Salvador, the Commissioners stated that they would not let themselves be pressured or impressed: they were after the objective truth and the hard facts.

The Commissioners and the group of professionals who collaborated with them in the investigations succeeded in overcoming obstacles and limitations that made it difficult to establish what had really happened, starting with the brief period of time—six months—afforded them under the Chapultepec Agreement. Given the magnitude of their task, this time frame, which seemed to stretch into Kafkaesque [suggestive of Franz Kafka, disorienting] infinity when they embarked upon their

A group of young men is lined up against a wall and searched by the Salvadoran Army during the unrest in San Salvador in the summer of 1980. © Keystone/Getty Images.

task, ultimately seemed meagre and barely sufficient to allow them to complete their work satisfactorily.

Throughout its mandate and while drafting its report, the Commission consistently sought to distance itself from events that had not been verified before it reached any conclusions. The whole of Salvadorian society, institutions and individuals familiar with acts of violence were invited to make them known to the Commission, under the guarantee of confidentiality and discretion provided for in the agreements. Paid announcements were placed in the press and on the radio and television to this end, and written and oral invitations were extended to the Parties to testify without restriction. Offices of the Commission were opened in various departmental capitals, including Chalatenango, Santa Ana and San Miguel. Written statements were taken, witnesses were heard, information from the sites of various incidents (e.g., El Calabozo, El Mozote, Sumpul River and Guancorita) was obtained. The Commission itself went to various departments with members of the professional team, occasionally travelling overland but more often in helicopters provided promptly and efficiently by ONUSAL [the UN observer mission]. As the investigation moved forward, it continued to yield new pieces of evidence: anyone who might have been involved was summonsed to testify without restriction as to time or place, usually in the Commission's offices or in secret locations, often outside El Salvador in order to afford witnesses greater protection.

The Commission maintained an "open-door" policy for hearing testimony and a "closed-door" policy for preserving confidentiality. Its findings illustrate the horrors of a war in which madness prevailed, and confirm beyond the shadow of a doubt that the incidents denounced, recorded and substantiated in this report actually took place. Whenever the Commission decided that its investigation of a specific case had yielded sufficient evidence, the matter was recorded in detail, with mention of the guilty parties. When it was determined that no further progress could be made for the time being, the corresponding documentation that was not subject to secrecy was delivered to the courts or else kept confidential until new information enabled it to be reactivated.

One fact must be squarely denounced: owing to the destruction or concealment of documents, or the failure to divulge the locations where numerous persons were imprisoned or bodies were buried, the burden of proof occasionally reverted to the Commission, the judiciary and citizens, who found themselves forced to reconstruct events. It will be up to those who administer the new system of justice to pursue these investigations and take whatever final decisions they consider appropriate at this moment in history.

Inevitably, the list of victims is incomplete: it was compiled on the basis of the complaints and testimony received and confirmed by the Commission.

Killers Tried to Justify Their Actions

The warped psychology engendered by the conflict led to a convulsion of violence. The civilian population in disputed or guerrilla controlled areas was automatically assumed to be the enemy, as at El Mozote and the Sumpul River. The opposing side behaved likewise, as when mayors were executed, the killings justified as acts of war because the victims had obstructed the delivery of supplies to combatants, or when defenceless pleasure-seekers became military targets, as in the case of the United States marines in the Zona Rosa of San Salvador. Meanwhile, the doctrine of national salvation and the principle of "he who is not for me is against me" were cited to ignore the neutrality, passivity and defencelessness of journalists and church workers, who served the community in various ways.

Such behaviour also led to the clandestine refinement of the death squads: the bullet which struck Monsignor Romero in the chest while he was celebrating mass on 24 March 1980 in a San Salvador church is a brutal symbol of the nightmare the country experienced during the war. And the murder of the six Jesuit priests 10 years later was the final outburst of the delirium that had infected the armed forces and the innermost recesses of certain government circles. The bullet in the portrait of Monsignor Romero, mute witness to this latest crime, repeats the nightmare image of those days.

Criminals Must Be Punished

It is a universally accepted premise that the individual is the subject of any criminal situation, since humans alone possess will and can therefore take decisions based on will: it is individuals that commit crimes, not the institutions they have created. As a result, it is to individuals and not their institutions that the corresponding penalties established by law must be applied.

However, there could be some situations in which the repetition of acts in time and space would seem to contradict the above premise. A situation of repeated criminal acts may arise

THE MAJORITY OF THE VIOLENCE STEMMED FROM THE GOVERNMENT

The independent Commission on the Truth for El Salvador registered 22,000 complaints of serious acts of political violence. The accused perpetrators of the violence are summarized below. The commission found that only 5 percent of the violence was committed by the left-wing guerillas.

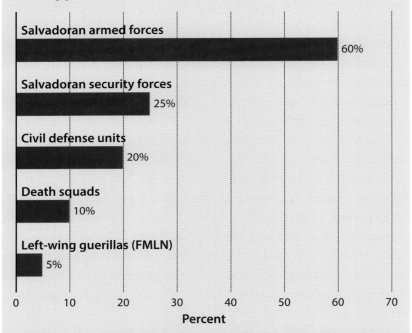

Salvadoran armed forces — 60%

Salvadoran security forces — 25%

Civil defense units — 20%

Death squads — 10%

Left-wing guerillas (FMLN) — 5%

Percent

Source: Commission on the Truth for El Salvador, *From Madness to Hope: The Twelve-Year War in El Salvador: Report of the Commission on the Truth for El Salvador*, 1993.

in which different individuals act within the same institution in unmistakably similar ways, independently of the political ideology of Governments and decision makers. This gives reason to believe that institutions may indeed commit crimes, if the same behaviour becomes a constant of the institution and, especially, if clear-cut accusations are met with a cover-up by the institution to which the accused belong and the institution is slow to act when investigations reveal who is responsible. In such circumstances, it is easy to succumb to the argument that repeated crimes mean that the institution is to blame.

The Commission on the Truth did not fall into that temptation: at the beginning of its mandate, it received hints from the highest level to the effect that institutions do not commit crimes and therefore that responsibilities must be established by naming names. At the end of its mandate, it again received hints from the highest level, this time to the opposite effect, namely, that it should not name names, perhaps in order to protect certain individuals in recognition of their genuine and commendable eagerness to help create situations which facilitated the peace agreements and national reconciliation.

However, the Commission believes that responsibility for anything that happened during the period of the conflict could not and should not be laid at the door of the institution, but rather of those who ordered the procedures for operating in the way that members of the institution did and also of those who, having been in a position to prevent such procedures, were compromised by the degree of tolerance and permissiveness with which they acted from their positions of authority or leadership or by the fact that they covered up incidents which came to their knowledge or themselves gave the order which led to the action in question. This approach protects institutions and punishes criminals. . . .

The Government Violated Humanitarian Law

With few exceptions, serious acts of violence prohibited by the rules of humanitarian law applicable to the Salvadorian conflict are also violations of the non-repealable provisions of the International Covenant on Civil and Political Rights and the American Convention on Human Rights, the two human rights treaties ratified by the State of El Salvador. The two instruments also prohibit derogation from any rights guaranteed in any humanitarian law treaty to which the State is a party.

As a result, neither the Salvadorian State nor persons acting on its behalf or in its place can claim that the existence of an armed conflict justified the commission of serious acts of violence in contravention of one or other of the human rights treaties mentioned above or of the applicable instruments of humanitarian law binding on the State.

In Guatemala, Government Forces Carried Out Large-Scale Killings

Encyclopedia of Race and Racism

In the following viewpoint, the Encyclopedia of Race and Racism *asserts that decades of armed conflict within Guatemala culminated in genocide committed by the country's military. The massacres of indigenous Guatemalans—primarily people of Mayan ancestry—reached a peak in the early 1980s, it explains. Overall, at least two hundred thousand people lost their lives. Lethal persecution of Mayans stretches back to the first European colonial period in the 1500s, the author states, and modern-day guerrilla groups evoked the historical injustice. However, the author argues, their opposition—the Guatemalan army—received substantial support, covertly and openly, from the United States.*

Genocide is the physical destruction of an ethnic group and the most extreme expression of racism. During the 1970s and 1980s, the Mayan people of Guatemala experienced a brutal genocide, perpetrated mainly by the Guatemalan state under a racist and terrorist policy designed to protect and strengthen the political and economic power of an embattled social elite.

This episode of genocide was part of the "Silent Holocaust" in Guatemala, which grew out of thirty-six years of internal armed conflict between different guerrilla organizations and the Guatemalan Army. The Commission for Historical Clarification, set up in 1996 to investigate "human rights violations and acts of violence linked to the period of armed conflict," has pointed out that this military confrontation had a high human cost for Guatemalan society as a whole. Nevertheless, 83 percent of the victims were Mayan civilians, predominantly older adults, children, and women.

The Guatemalan state forces were responsible for 91 percent of the total human rights violations and genocidal acts, while guerrilla organizations accounted for around 3 percent. A trilogy of genocidal campaigns—named "Scorched Earth," "Model Villages," and "CPR Persecution"—were introduced by the Guatemalan Army between 1981 and 1983. These campaigns clearly demonstrated the racism and cruelty inherent in the application of counter-insurgency forces.

In December 1996, a peace accord was signed by the government of Guatemala and the *Unidad Revolucionaria Nacional Guatemalteca* (Guatemalan National Revolutionary Unity, or URNG), and a fragile peace process began, which at least stopped the prolongation of the conflict. The two sides committed to resolving the causes that triggered the conflict and initiating the painful process of reconstructing and understanding the recent historical events.

Mayans Were Targets for Centuries

Guatemala is a small Central American country characterized by its extraordinary geography and great ethnic and linguistic diversity, reflected in its indigenous populations of Mayan, Xinca, and Garífuna people. This cultural mosaic comprises more than half of the population of Guatemala, estimated at 12 million inhabitants. The Ladino population (mixed Amerindian-Spanish heritage) constitutes the other half. The multicultural composition of Guatemalan society is the fruit of a millennial civilizing process, which had its beginnings with the splendor of the Mayan civilization that flowered about 1500 B.C. The European invasion of America, beginning in the sixteenth century, began the first genocide in this region, destroying Mayan peoples and cultures and putting their societies under a colonial system.

Yet after three centuries of Spanish colonization, the indigenous peoples miraculously survived the genocide and ethnocide perpetrated by both the conservative and liberal states of the nation, which had excluded them from the national project and reduced them to laborers on the great plantations.

The triumph of the 1944 "October Revolution" in Guatemala began a democratic, national modernization process that implemented deep social reforms, such as the promulgation of a new constitution, labor legislation, and agrarian reform. However, agrarian reform adversely affected North American economic interests and invited retaliation, especially from the United Fruit Company.

The North American intervention in Guatemala in June 1954 marked the beginning of the first U.S. Central Intelligence Agency (CIA) operations in Latin America, which were in line with the general anticommunist policy adopted during the cold war. The Commission for Historical Clarification points out that following the counter revolutionary triumph of General Carlos Castillo Armas on July 8, 1954, Guatemala began a period of historical regression that provoked the causes of the genocidal violence of the late twentieth century.

The first guerrilla attacks in Guatemala began during the 1960s in the East, on the South Coast, and in Guatemala City, all nonindigenous regions. The first guerrilla organizations, such as the *Movimiento Revolucionario 13 de Noviembre* (November 13th Revolutionary Movement, or MR-13), *Frente 20 de Octubre* (October 20th Front), and later the *Fuerzas Armadas Rebeldes* (Rebel Armed Forces, or FAR), implemented a *guerrilla focus* strategy, inspired by the Cuban revolution of 1959.

In 1965, the Guatemalan army initiated a ferocious counter-insurgency campaign that prevailed against the guerrillas. The new *Doctrina de Seguridad Nacional* (National Security Doctrine, or DSN) implemented a new and more modern counterinsurgency method that resulted in more than 8,000 victims, mostly civilians.

Guerillas Push for National Liberation

The Commission for Historical Clarification has concluded that the beginning of the violence in Guatemala was the result of racist and exclusionary national policies, which made it impossible for the state to achieve a social consensus in Guatemalan society.

During the 1970s, a number of guerrilla groups emerged in the Mayan region, including the *Organización del Pueblo en Armas* (Organization of the People in Arms, or ORPA), which appeared in 1971. The following year, the *Ejército Guerrillero de los Pobres* (Guerrilla Army of the Poor, or EGP) arose in the Guatemalan Highlands. The FAR was decimated in the 1960s, but resumed its military actions in 1979. After suffering ferocious political persecution and kidnappings, the *Partido Guatemalteco del Trabajo* (Guatemalan Labor Party, or PGT) decided to participate in the armed warfare in 1979.

The military-political strategy adopted by the new guerrilla groups sought to incorporate the indigenous masses into what was becoming a war of national liberation. They considered that the previous guerrilla experience had largely failed, partly because they had been forced to limit their operations to discrete geographic areas in eastern Guatemala, a region populated mostly by Ladinos.

A major earthquake struck Guatemala in 1976. This natural disaster caused a social cataclysm that demonstrated the corruption of the state, as well as its limited capacity to respond to a disaster and organize a response. In the following years, numerous social organizations arose in Guatemala, mainly cooperatives and unions that mobilized protests of various kinds against the violence and repression and that fought for better labor conditions, wages, and benefits.

The State Kills Entire Mayan Villages

In response to this emergent social movement, the state unfolded a counterinsurgency plan that intensified repression and violence. Beginning in 1980, state forces increased the practices of "kidnappings" and "disappearances" against union leaders, university students and faculty, and political candidates. Violence against the Mayan people took the form of "selective murders" of community leaders. The Commission for Historical Clarification has provided evidence that at least 100 Mayan community leaders were assassinated in Chajul, Cotzal, and Nebaj between February of 1976 and November of 1977.

As this repression increased, the first massacres of Mayan communities began. In 1980, in Panzós, a Q'eqchí community in the department of Baja Verapaz, 150 *kaibiles,* or military elites, assassinated more than 300 farmers in the town square. This action was in response to Q'eqchí peasants making claims to lands that had been alienated by military officials and plantations owners.

The *Comité de Unidad Campesina* (Campesino Unity Committee, or CUC) founded in the mid 1980s by Mayan farmer leaders and poor Ladinos, soon initiated a series of strikes, both as a strategy to gain better labor conditions and as a protest against the violence. By January 1981, CUC leaders had peacefully occupied the Spanish Embassy, enabling them to make their protests heard outside the country. This mobilization ended when state forces burned the embassy killing more than thirty people. That same year, CUC members organized a meeting in Tecpán, in the department of Chimaltenango, and wrote the Declaration of Iximche, which denounced the oppression, exclusion, racism, and cultural intolerance in Guatemala. At about this time, the Catholic Diocese of the El Quiche department was closed due to acts of repression against its members.

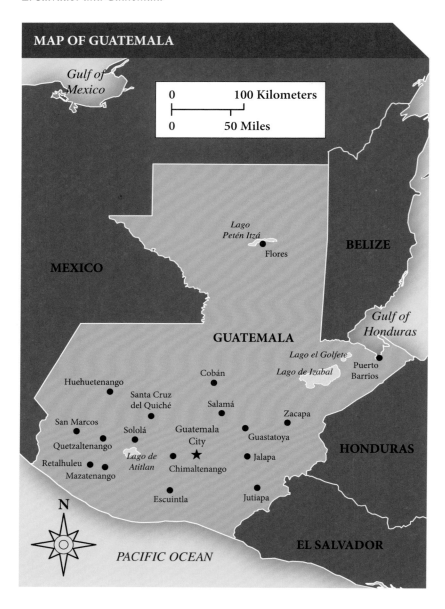

MAP OF GUATEMALA

In 1980 the four guerrilla organizations, encouraged by the triumph of the 1979 Sandinista revolution in Nicaragua and the apparently weak position of the Guatemalan Army, spread its military operations over a vast geographic area. This move has since been viewed as a serious military mistake, for the army was well prepared to confront the guerrilla organizations and had already planned its genocidal military campaigns in response. Previous to the military counteroffensive (between July and August 1981), the Guatemalan Army managed to capture all the "secure houses" of the ORPA and the EGP in Guatemala City. Although military aid from the United States had been suspended indefinitely due to increased human rights violations, the Guatemalan Army still managed to receive military aid approved years before.

The "Scorched Earth" Plan Was Genocidal

In the middle of 1981, the government of President Lucas Garcia began a military counter-offensive plan designated "Ash 81." This operation was in fact a well-planned genocide against the Mayan peoples, who were accused of being "communists" and supporting the rebel groups, thereby justifying the campaign called "Scorched Earth."

The main objective of this genocidal campaign was to "drain the water to the fish"—that is, to isolate the guerrillas from the civil population, and thus from their base of support. The anthropologist Robert Carmack, in *Harvest of Violence: The Maya Indians and the Guatemalan Crisis* (1988) points out that the military intelligence was used to draw a map demarcating the different communities with different colors. Each color designated the military actions to be made, depending on the political proximity of each community to the guerrillas. The "Green" communities were considered "free" of the "internal enemy." Those communities where some persons or leaders were believed to be supporting the guerrillas were designated as "Pink" or "Yellow." In these areas the army applied a selective repression, including "kidnappings," "disappearances," and "killings" of social leaders and "suspects." "Red" communities were selected for total destruction because there was intelligence information that they were fully supporting the guerrillas.

The racism and code colors significantly helped the Gua-temalan Army, mostly directed by Ladinos, in the conception and planning of this genocide. The "Scorched Earth" military campaign that followed began with the taking of the city of Chimaltenango and other strategic places in order to surround the "internal enemy."

The guerrillas were not able to stop the bloody military coun-teroffensive of the Guatemalan Army, despite the fact that they had about 6,000 combatants and a base of support exceeding 250,000 people. Forty-five massacres were committed by the Guatemalan Army from March 1981 to March 1982, with 1,678 victims. The average number of victims per massacre was 37.29 people.

The "Scorched Earth" military campaign was directed by the High Guatemalan Commander using "kaibiles," or elite forces, and Mayans that were forcibly recruited. Once military control had been gained over the populations that had not been de-stroyed, the Guatemalan Army organized the *Patrullas de Auto-defensa Civil* (Civil Self-Defense Patrols, or PACs) in order to "take care of" the population and defend the community from the threat of communism.

The army intelligence apparatus and a mechanism of social control were increased, using military commissioners, the po-lice, customs guards, and secret agents, who conducted a "witch hunt" against those who protested the violence. The G-2 (mili-tary intelligence) used paid informants, or "orejas," to gain intel-ligence about the guerrilla groups.

Cruelty Marked the "Model Villages" Plan

In 1982 the government of Lucas Garcia was overthrown in a coup d'état that made General Efraín Ríos Montt the new presi-dent. Ríos Montt then inaugurated a new military plan, "Victory 82," with well-directed and improved military actions. This geno-cide campaign promised to "eliminate," "annihilate," and "exter-minate" the "internal enemy" very quickly and "gain the hearts of the population."

From March 1982 to March 1983, thirty-two selective massacres were carried out, killing 1,424 people. The massacre in Plan de Sánchez in Rabinal, Alta Verapaz, claimed the lives of children, women, and the elderly. The Inter-American Commission on Human Rights in its Report 31/99, Case 11.763 Plan de Sánchez, Guatemala, describes this massacre as follows:

> Early on the morning of July 18, 1982, two grenades fell to the east and west of Plan de Sánchez. A group of approximately 60 men dressed in military uniforms and armed with assault rifles, and four "judiciales" allegedly arrived in Plan de Sánchez between 2:00 and 3:00 P.M. Those four judiciales were identified by witnesses, and the two officials in charge were identified as Lieutenants Solares and Díaz. The petitioners report that soldiers monitored points of entry into the community, while others went house to house rounding up the population. Girls and young women were held in one location, while older women, men and children were gathered in another. Approximately 20 girls between 12 and 20 years of age were taken to one house where they were raped and then killed. The rest of the population was forced into another house and the adjoining patio. The petitioners allege that, at about 5:00 P.M., soldiers threw two hand grenades into that house, and then sprayed it and the patio with sustained gunfire. Small children were hit or kicked to death. Shots were reportedly heard in another location, where four bodies were later found. The petitioners describe the soldiers as having subsequently set fire to the house where the majority of the victims had been killed before leaving the community some hours later.

The extreme cruelty of these military actions against a non-combatant population, as well as various atrocities, such as the extraction of the viscera of victims who were still alive or the opening of the wombs of pregnant women, demonstrate the genocide and racism of this period. Thousands of Maya fled from Guatemala seeking refuge in Mexico, while others fled from the army into the mountains to join the *Comunidades y*

Pueblos en Resistencia (Communities of Populations in Resistance, or CPRs).

Ríos Montt's military campaign was more selective than its predecessor, and the number of victims per massacre was increased. Victoria Sanford, in her book *Buried Secrets* (2003), has pointed out that the percentage of victims per massacre was increased from 37.29 during Lucas Garcia's regime to fifty. Ríos Montt introduced new military projects for civilians, the "Model Villages." These were very similar to the "Strategic Hamlets" program implemented by the U.S. Army during the Vietnam War. Thousands of Mayans were forced to live in the model villages, which were under permanent military control by the Guatemalan Army.

The government of Ríos Montt also implemented the "Fusiles y Frijoles" (guns and beans), and "Techo, Trabajo y Tortillas" (roof, work and tortillas) policies as part of the counter-insurgency project. Through these policies, the Guatemalan Army offered protection and assistance to Mayan civilians in exchange of their incorporation to the PACs. In addition, the Special Privilege Tribunal was created to punish the political opponents in summary judgments. As a result of these policies, the guerrilla organizations, realizing their weakened condition, saw the urgent necessity to reorganize. In February of 1982, the four guerrilla organizations reunited to form *Unidad Revolucionaria National Guatemalteca* (Guatemalan National Revolutionary Unity, or URNG).

Another Campaign Expands the Killing

The genocidal atrocities committed during the Ríos Montt regime ended in August 1983, when Montt was deposed by another coup d'état. The new president, General Oscar Mejía Víctores, promised a transition to democracy and the end of armed conflict. Nevertheless, his government implemented another military plan, denominated "Firmness 83," whose main objective was the removal of the last "resistance focus" of the guerrillas

Police and armed members of a Civil Defense Patrol stand outside a church in a "model village" near Nebaj, Guatemala. Model villages were one of the Guatemalan Army's counterinsurgency strategies that resulted in the mass killings of Mayans. © Cindy Karp/Time & Life Pictures/ Getty Images.

and the destruction of the CPRs, who still miraculously survived in the mountains and jungle. The Guatemalan Army succeeded by isolating the civilian population from the guerrillas and by "annihilating," "exterminating," and "destroying" several Mayan communities. The "Scorched Earth," "Model Villages" and "Persecution of the CPRs" genocide campaigns helped the army dominate the military confrontation with the guerrillas.

Reduced in number, without their support base, and crowded into a reduced geographic area, the guerrillas also suffered a "surgical attack" from the Guatemalan Army. Though they still maintained a considerable number of members, there was no real possibility that they could challenge the army.

The control of the population through the Civil Self-Defense Patrols (PACs), the Model Villages program, military commissioners, and military intelligence was also crucial in this process. The Commission for Historical Clarification points out that at least a million Mayan people were forced to belong to PACs by 1983. In 1984, under the military plan known as "Re-Encounter 84," a new Constitutional Assembly was created that initiated the work of elaborating a new constitution.

In 1985, the plan "National Stability 1985" was implemented, allowing a new presidential election to be held. The victor was Vinicio Cerezo, the Christian Democratic Party candidate. The Guatemalan leftist organizations did not participate in this election, however, and the URNG actively boycotted it. In an effort to end military hostilities, Cerezo initiated a dialogue with the guerrillas in Madrid in October 1987. The Esquipulas I and II meetings, held under the mediation of the Mexican government, gave an impulse to the peace process. During the dialogue process, numerous nongovernmental organizations arose and began to demand land, respect for human rights, a search for "disappeared," the return of refugees, and indigenous peoples' rights. They formed the *Coordinadora Nacional de las Viudas de Guatemala* (National Coordination of Guatemalan Widows, or CONAVIGUA), the *Grupo de Ayuda Mutua* (Mutual Support

Group, or GAM), the Vicente Menchú and Myrna Mack foundations, and the *Academia de Lenguas Mayas* (Mayan Languages Academy, or ALM), among other groups.

Peace accords between the government of Guatemala and the URNG were finally signed in December of 1996 after years of negotiation. Since then, advances in the peace agenda have been minimal, despite efforts by the United Nations Verification Mission in Guatemala (MINUGUA) and the *Secretaría de la Paz* (Secretariat for Peace, or SEPAZ), creating conditions for new social conflicts, particularly in the matters of land, human rights, and labor.

The Toll Was Massive

The Commission for Historical Clarification has provided evidence that the human cost of this tragedy includes the 626 Mayan communities destroyed by fire, 200,000 people assassinated or "disappeared," 1.5 million people displaced, 150,000 refugees who fled to Mexico, and several hundred people exiled into other countries.

There is evidence that 91 percent of the violations to the human rights and genocidal acts were committed by the state forces and that 83 percent of the victims were Mayan people. This evidence comes from first-hand accounts, such as that of Rigoberta Menchú, a survivor of the massacres and a Nobel Prize winner in 1992; from the human rights report *Guatemala: Nunca Más (Guatemala: Never More, 1998)*; from the Interdiocesan Project for the Recuperation of Historical Memory (1998); and from the Commission for Historical Clarification, with the support of the United Nations.

The Guatemalan state participated in genocide, a crime against humanity forbidden by the UN Convention for the Prevention of the Crime of Genocide. The massacres perpetrated against noncombatant populations demonstrate the barbarity and racism of the state during this period. The state also participated in ethnocide, the destruction of Mayan culture in the form of ceremonial centers, language, dress, systems of authority, and exercise of spirituality.

Lamentably, public knowledge of this truth has provoked more victims. For example, Monsignor Juan Gerardi, a Catholic archbishop and the main force behind the report *Guatemala: Never More*, was assassinated two days after the publication of the report. In addition, as of 2007, none of those responsible for these acts has yet faced justice, despite the judgments that have been made against them.

US Policy in Guatemala, 1966–1996

Kate Doyle and Carlos Osorio

In the following viewpoint, two researchers assert that top-secret dispatches from Guatemala reveal the extent of US involvement in the Guatemalan genocide. By 1966, when the dispatches begin, US advisory participation was under way, the authors maintain. According to the authors, some US officials on the scene saw that the Guatemalan government was going far beyond ethical standards, yet they continued to work with the country's leaders. Kate Doyle is a senior analyst and director of the Guatemala Documentation Project at the National Security Archive, and Carlos Osorio is a senior research associate.

Document 1
[*U.S. Counter-Terror Assistance to Guatemalan Security Forces*]
January 4, 1966
United States Agency for International Development,
Secret cable

Kate Doyle and Carlos Osorio, "US Policy in Guatemala, 1966–1996," *National Security Archive Electronic Briefing Book*. These materials are reproduced from www.nsarchive.org with the permission of the National Security Archive.

U.S. Public Safety Advisor John Longan, on temporary loan from his post in Venezuela, assists the Guatemalan government in establishing an urban counter-terrorist task force in the wake of a rash of kidnappings for ransom by insurgent organizations. During meetings with senior military and police officials, Longan advises how to establish overt and covert operations in Guatemala, to include designing "frozen area plans" for police raids, setting up new road blocks within the capital, and creating a "safe house" in the Presidential Palace to centralize information gathered on the kidnappings. Longan also addresses the role of U.S. military advisors, the sale of U.S. supplies and equipment to the Guatemalan armed forces and Col. Peralta's national address offering cash rewards for top communist leaders—dead or alive. [Note: CAS is an acronym for "Covert Action Section," the operational arm of the CIA station.]

Document 2
[*Death List*]
March 1966
Central Intelligence Agency, Secret cable

The CIA Station in Guatemala City reports the secret execution of several Guatemalan "communists and terrorists" by Guatemalan authorities on the night of March 6, 1966. The victims—the leader of the Partido Guatemalteco de Trabajadores (PGT), Victor Manuel Gutiérrez, among them—are several of the more than two dozen PGT members and associates abducted, tortured and killed by Guatemalan security forces in March of 1966. The incident became famous as the first case of forced mass "disappearance" in Guatemala's history.

Document 3
Request for Special Training
December 3, 1966
Department of State, Secret cable

U.S. Deputy Chief of Mission in Guatemala Viron Vaky forwards to Washington the text of a cable the embassy received from the SouthCom Commander-in-Chief, Gen. Porter. Porter's cable describes a request made to him by the Guatemalan Vice Defense Minister, Col. Francisco Sosa Avila, for U.S. assistance in the covert training of special kidnapping squads that would target leftists. Although Porter declines, he does not hesitate to recommend that the United States "fully support current police improvement programs and initiate military psychological warfare training and additional counterinsurgency operations training." Vaky is troubled.

Document 4
Guatemala: A Counter-Insurgency Running Wild?
October 23, 1967
Department of State, Secret intelligence note

The Bureau of Intelligence and Research questions the current Guatemalan government's ability to control military and police forces in light of "accumulating evidence that the counter-insurgency machine is out of control." The document describes some of the methods utilized in Guatemala's "successful" campaign, including the formation of clandestine counter-terrorist units to carry out abductions, bombings, torture, and summary executions "of real and alleged communists."

Document 5
Guatemala and Counter-Terror
March 29, 1968
Department of State, Secret memorandum

Viron Vaky, back in Washington with the State Department's Policy Planning Council, writes an extraordinary indictment of U.S. policy in Guatemala in a memorandum to the Assistant Secretary of State for Inter-American Affairs, Covey Oliver. Vaky argues that the Guatemalan government's use of counter-terror is

Families of massacred Mayans carry coffins during a mass reburial in Zacualpa, Guatemala, on April 19, 2002. Similar reburials of victims' remains took place in Guatemala as mass graves were found. © Andrea Nieto/Getty Images.

indiscriminate and brutal, and has impeded modernization and institution building within the country. Furthermore, he writes, the United States has condoned such tactics. "This is not only because we have concluded we cannot do anything about it, for we never really tried. Rather we suspected that maybe it is a good tactic, and that as long as Communists are being killed it is alright. Murder, torture and mutilation are alright if our side is doing it and the victims are Communists." Vaky urges a new policy in Guatemala that rejects "counter-terror" as an accepted tactic and represents a "clear ethical stand" on the part of the United States.

Document 6
Guatemalan Antiterrorist Campaign
January 12, 1971
Defense Intelligence Agency, Secret intelligence bulletin

In the midst of what becomes a year-long state of siege imposed by President Carlos Arana Osorio, Guatemalan security forces "quietly eliminated" hundreds of "terrorists and bandits," mainly in the countryside. In Guatemala City, police apprehend or kill about 30 suspected subversives, including a senior Communist Party member. The army has also closed all roads leading from the capital and is conducting house-to-house searches for suspects. . . .

Document 8
Internal Security: "Death Squad" Strikes
February 4, 1974
Department of State, Secret cable

Cable alerts Washington to the resurgence of "death squad" activity. The clandestine organization, Escuadron de la Muerte, has resumed its activities with the shooting of six alleged criminals. Earlier executions were carried out in the name of the "Avenging Vulture" (Buitre Justiciero), which government sources told the embassy was a "smoke-screen" for police extra-legal activities. The current killings have all the signs of another police operation. . . .

Document 13
Guatemala: What Next?
October 5, 1981
Department of State, Secret memorandum

An assessment from the State Department's Human Rights Bureau of President Lucas Garcia's repressive policies and the response the United States should take. The memo asserts that Lucas is convinced that continued repression is the only successful way to combat the guerrilla movement, and that he will probably continue this campaign with or without U.S. security assistance. "If Lucas is right and the GOG can successfully 'go it alone' in its policy of repression, there is no need for the U.S. to provide the GOG with redundant political and military support." The memo counsels State to adopt a wait-and-see attitude.

Document 14
[*Counterinsurgency Operations in El Quiché*]
February 1982
Central Intelligence Agency, Secret cable

The massacres continue. This cable from the CIA Station documents a Guatemalan army "sweep" operation through the Ixil Triangle in El Quiché. The aim of the operation is to destroy all towns and villages suspected of supporting the Guerrilla Army of the Poor (EGP). Those who collaborate with the military are allowed shelter and food in refugee camps. If there is resistance from anyone in a town, the entire town is considered hostile and destroyed; if a village is abandoned before the military arrive, it is also considered hostile and is destroyed. According to the cable, the army has yet to encounter any major guerrilla force in the area and its successes are limited to the destruction of entire villages and the killing of Indians suspected of collaborating or sympathizing with the rebels. "The well-documented belief by the army that the entire Ixil Indian population is pro-EGP has created a situation in which the army can be expected to give no quarter to combatants and non-combatants alike." . . .

Document 16
Analysis of Human Rights Reports on Guatemala by Amnesty International, WOLA/NISGUA, and Guatemala Human Rights Commission
October 22, 1982
Department of State, Confidential cable

After analyzing human rights reporting on Guatemala from Amnesty International, the Washington Office on Latin America, the Network in Solidarity with Guatemala and the Guatemalan Human Rights Commission, the U.S. Embassy concludes that "a concerted disinformation campaign" is being waged against the Guatemalan government in the U.S. "by groups supporting the communist insurgency in Guatemala." It accuses the groups of assigning responsibility for atrocities to the army without sufficient evidence, abuses which may have never occurred or may have been propagated by guerrillas. While the cable concedes that the army has committed violations, it concludes that many of the accusations by the human rights organizations are unfounded and that their sources are highly questionable, since they come from "well-known communist front groups." It questions the fact that these reports did not use the Guatemalan government as a source and that they failed to charge guerrilla groups with human rights violations.

Document 17
Guatemala: Reports of Atrocities Mark Army Gains
Circa late-1982
Department of State, Secret report

Description of the scorched earth campaigns. The "rifles and beans" policy initiated in July by President Efraín Ríos Montt is characterized by alternating the use of carrots—through amnesty for the guerrillas—and sticks—through the state of siege, a heavy military offensive and the organization of Indians into Civil Defense Forces. The government has heightened its control over rural areas through the construction of strategic hamlets for local communities. There are widespread allegations of massacres, rape and mayhem by the troops. "The Embassy does not as yet believe that there is sufficient evidence to link government troops to any of the reported massacres." . . .

Document 25
Stop Delivery of Military Assistance to Guatemala
December 16, 1990
Department of State, Secret cable

In the wake of the murder of American citizen Michael DeVine, the Bush administration decides to freeze the delivery of security assistance to Guatemala. The cable states that the Cerezo government intends to "string the investigation out, as it has on all past cases, until it leaves office in three weeks. This is unacceptable." The United States will wait to deal with a new government in the hope that progress can then be made in the DeVine case and other outstanding human rights cases.

Note: In 1995, U.S. press reports revealed that although overt U.S. military aid was indeed halted in December 1990, millions of dollars of secret CIA funds continued to flow to the Guatemalan armed forces during the ensuing years. Those funds were finally cut off after they became public.

Document 26
Selective Violence Paralyzes the Left
May 10, 1991
Department of State, Secret cable

A General with US–Backing Faces Genocide Charges

Efraín Ríos Montt (1926–) is one of the most controversial men in Guatemala. He came to power in 1982 in a military coup, declared himself president, was ousted about a year later, yet remained prominent in the national legislature for decades afterward. His presidency came during the height of the country's armed conflict. Later, after years of procedural arguments, Ríos Montt was indicted in 2012 on genocide charges.

Supporters saw him as a strong leader against rebels who were threatening the country. Those supporters included many US officials; as a young man, Ríos Montt received substantial US military training, and he remained connected with the CIA over the years. President Ronald Reagan praised him as dedicated to democracy.

He was almost elected president of Guatemala in 1974. He blamed his defeat in part on a campaign by left-wing Catholic priests. In his later years, Ríos Montt made several more unsuccessful attempts to become president. In 1978, before seizing presidential power, he declared himself a born-again Christian Protestant. His brother Mario became a Catholic bishop and eventually head of the human rights commission that investigated, among other things, atrocities committed under his brother's leadership.

Ambassador Thomas Stroock describes the strategy, tactics and modus operandi behind a recent campaign of terror waged by the Archivos, D-2 and other military and police death squads. The wave of selective violence—which over the year killed anthropologist Myrna Mack Chang and political activist Dinora Pérez, among others—is being used by security forces to spread fear among the targeted organizations and individuals. "It is not clear the President [Serrano Elías] openly opposes actions against the left, particularly while there is a war on. He seems ambiguous on the topic, an ambiguity that fuels the violence. . . . We conclude, given the ideological bent of the president and most of those closest to him, that the current GOG may look with benign [regard] upon efforts physically to eliminate the left as a remotely potential rival to power." . . .

Document 29
Concerns Over the Military
December 21, 1993
Department of State, Secret cable

The Clinton administration's newly-confirmed ambassador to Guatemala, Marilyn McAfee, expresses concern that U.S. human rights policies—including pressure exerted in the DeVine case and conditions imposed on continued IMET—are alienating the Guatemalan military. McAfee fears that anger over U.S. policy may work to the advantage of military hard-liners and undermine the moderate, Minister of Defense René Enríquez and, by extension, President de León Carpio. "We must try and calibrate our actions to build and retain the confidence of the army."

Document 30
Suspected Presence of Clandestine Cemeteries on a Military Installation
April 11, 1994
Defense Intelligence Agency, Secret message

Reviews new information about the Guatemalan military's use of the southern air base in Retalhuleu during the mid-1980s. According to the document, the army's intelligence directorate (D-2) coordinated the counterinsurgency campaign in southwest Guatemala from this base, using it both as an operations post and an interrogation center. Small buildings used as interrogation rooms and pits filled with water used to hold captured suspects once existed on the base; they have since been destroyed or filled in with concrete. The document describes the army's technique of disposing bodies (and, at times, live prisoners) by flying them over the ocean and pushing them out of a plane. "In this way, the D-2 has been able to remove the majority of evidence showing that the prisoners had been tortured and killed." Document also reports that the base contains clandestine burial sites. . . .

The Guatemalan Government Committed Genocide

Guatemalan Commission for Historical Clarification

In the following viewpoint, an independent commission concludes that Guatemala's government, its military, and others in power carried out a range of human rights violations, including genocide, against Mayan communities and other segments of Guatemala's population. The commission's report condemns executions, the use of lawless death squads, and rape. The commission asserts that the brutality also attacked the cultural rights of the Mayan people. The commission attributes only 7 percent of serious violations to anti-government guerrillas. The Guatemalan Commission for Historical Clarification was created in 1994 during the country's peace negotiations and was headed by Christian Tomuschat, a German law professor.

Those acts which are directly attributable to the State include those perpetrated by its public servants and state agencies. Additionally, the State holds direct responsibility for the actions of civilians to whom it delegated, *de jure* or *de facto* [in the law or in fact], authority to act on its behalf, or with its consent, acquiescence or knowledge. This includes military commissioners who

Guatemalan Commission for Historical Clarification, "Guatemala: Memory of Silence," 1999.

were by law, agents of military authority; Civil Patrol members, insofar as the military authorities organised, directed or ordered them or had knowledge of their actions; the large land-owners who were granted police functions by the 1936 Penal Code; and any other third party that may have acted under the direction or with the knowledge of state agents.

The State must also respond for breaches in the legal obligation to investigate, try and punish human right violations, even when these were not committed directly by state agents or when the State may not have had initial knowledge of them.

Human rights violations and acts of violence attributable to actions by the State represent 93% of those registered by the CEH [the commission]; they demonstrate that human rights violations caused by state repression were repeated, and that, although varying in intensity, were prolonged and continuous, being especially severe from 1978 to 1984, a period during which 91% of the violations documented by the CEH were committed. Eighty-five percent of all cases of human rights violations and acts of violence registered by the CEH are attributable to the Army, acting either alone or in collaboration with another force, and 18%, to the Civil Patrols, which were organised by the armed forces.

The Government Used the National Security Doctrine to Justify the Massacres

Using the National Security Doctrine as its justification, and acting in the name of anti-communism, crimes were committed which include the kidnapping and assassination of political activists, students, trade unionists and human rights advocates, all categorised as "subversives"; the forced disappearance of political and social leaders and poor peasants; and the systematic use of torture.

During most of the internal armed confrontation, attempts to form organisations for the defence of human rights resulted in the elimination of their leaders. In the 1980s, the appearance of new groups of human rights defenders in various areas was received by the State with intensive repression which resulted in the murder or disappearance of many of their members. Campaigns directed towards discrediting this type of organisation, presenting them as "subversive", were one of the constants of the repression.

The Army's perception of Mayan communities as natural allies of the guerrillas contributed to increasing and aggravating the human rights violations perpetrated against them, demonstrating an aggressive racist component of extreme cruelty that led to the extermination en masse of defenceless Mayan communities purportedly linked to the guerrillas—including children, women and the elderly—through methods whose cruelty has outraged the moral conscience of the civilised world.

These massacres and the so-called scorched earth operations, as planned by the State, resulted in the complete extermination of many Mayan communities, along with their homes, cattle, crops and other elements essential to survival. The CEH registered 626 massacres attributable to these forces.

The CEH has noted particularly serious cruelty in many acts committed by agents of the State, especially members of the Army, in their operations against Mayan communities. The counterinsurgency strategy not only led to violations of basic human rights, but also to the fact that these crimes were committed with particular cruelty, with massacres representing their archetypal form. In the majority of massacres there is evidence of multiple acts of savagery, which preceded, accompanied or occurred after the deaths of the victims. Acts such as the killing of defenceless children, often by beating them against walls or throwing them alive into pits where the corpses of adults were later thrown; the amputation of limbs; the impaling of victims; the killing of persons by covering them in petrol and burning them alive; the extraction, in the presence of others, of the viscera of victims who were still alive; the confinement of people who had been mortally tortured, in agony for days; the opening of the wombs of pregnant women, and other similarly atrocious acts, were not only actions of extreme cruelty against the victims, but also morally degraded the perpetrators and those who inspired, ordered or tolerated these actions.

During the armed confrontation the cultural rights of the Mayan people were also violated. The Army destroyed ceremonial centres, sacred places and cultural symbols. Language and dress, as well as other elements of cultural identification, were targets of repression. Through the militarization of the communities, the establishment of the PAC [civil patrols] and the military commissioners, the legitimate authority structure of the communities was broken; the use of their own norms and procedures to regulate social life and resolve conflicts was prevented; the exercise of Mayan spirituality and the Catholic religion was obstructed, prevented or repressed; the maintenance and development of the indigenous peoples' way of life and their system of social organisation was upset. Displacement and refuge exacerbated the difficulties of practising their own culture.

The Systematic Use of Disappearances, Executions, Rape, and Death Squads

The CEH has concluded that in Guatemala forced disappearance was a systematic practise which in nearly all cases was the result of intelligence operations. The objective was to disarticulate the movements or organisations identified by the State as favourable to the insurgency, as well as to spread terror among the people. The victims of these disappearances were peasants, social and student leaders, professors, political leaders, members of religious communities and priests, and even members of military or paramilitary organisations that fell under suspicion of collaborating with the enemy. Those responsible for these forced disappearances violated fundamental human rights.

The CEH concludes that the Guatemalan State repeatedly and systematically violated the right to life, through what this Report has called arbitrary executions. In many cases this was

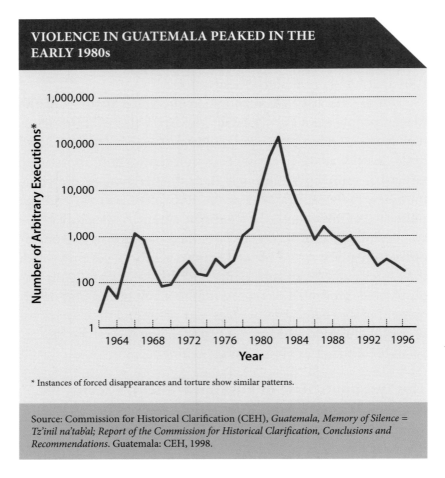

VIOLENCE IN GUATEMALA PEAKED IN THE EARLY 1980s

* Instances of forced disappearances and torture show similar patterns.

Source: Commission for Historical Clarification (CEH), *Guatemala, Memory of Silence = Tz'inil na'tab'al; Report of the Commission for Historical Clarification, Conclusions and Recommendations.* Guatemala: CEH, 1998.

aggravated by extreme irreverence, as for instance, in situations in which the corpses were abandoned with evident indications of torture, mutilation, multiple bullet holes or burn marks. The perpetrators of these violations were Army officers, specialists and troops, death squads that either operated under the protection of the authorities or with members of these authorities, members of the Civil Patrols or military commissioners, and in certain cases, private individuals, specifically large land owners, with the consent or direct collaboration of state authorities.

The CEH's investigation has demonstrated that the rape of women, during torture or before being murdered, was a common practice aimed at destroying one of the most intimate and vulnerable aspects of the individual's dignity. The majority of rape victims were Mayan women. Those who survived the crime still suffer profound trauma as a result of this aggression, and the communities themselves were deeply offended by this practice. The presence of sexual violence in the social memory of the communities has become a source of collective shame.

Some of the human rights violations were committed by means of covert operations. The military had clandestine units called "commandos" or "special squads" whose supplies, vehicles, arms, funding and operational instructions were provided by the regular structures of the Army, especially military intelligence. The work of these squads not only included execution and kidnapping, but also the development of counterinsurgency tactics of psychological war, propaganda and intimidation.

"Death squads" were also used; these were initially criminal groups made up of private individuals who enjoyed the tolerance and complicity of state authorities. The CEH has arrived at the well-founded presumption that, later, various actions committed by these groups were a consequence of decisions by the Army command, and that the composition of the death squads varied over time as members of the military were incorporated, until they became, in some cases, authentic clandestine military units. Their objective was to eliminate alleged members, allies or collaborators of the "subversives" using the help of civilians and lists prepared by military intelligence. The various names of the better known "death squads", such as, MANO (National Organised Action Movement), also known as Mano Blanca (White Hand) because of its logo, NOA (New Anti-Communist Organisation), CADEG (Anti-Communist Council of Guatemala), Ojo por Ojo (Eye for an Eye) and Jaguar Justiciero (Jaguar of Justice) and ESA (Secret Anti-Communist Army), were simply the transient names of the clandestine military units whose purpose was to eliminate the alleged members, allies or collaborators of "subversion".

The Legal System Failed

The courts were incapable of investigating, trying, judging and punishing even a small number of those responsible for the most serious human rights crimes, or of providing protection for the victims. This conclusion can be applied both to military tribunals charged with the investigation and punishment of crimes committed by individuals within their special jurisdiction, as well as to the ordinary justice system; the former, because it was part of the military apparatus involved in the confrontation, and the latter, because it had given up exercising its functions of protecting and safeguarding the rights of the individual.

Acts and omissions by the judicial branch, such as the systematic denial of *habeas corpus*, continuous interpretation of the law favourable to the authorities, indifference to the torture of detainees and limitations on the right to defence demonstrated the judges' lack of independence. These constituted grave violations of the right to due process and serious breaches of the State's duty to investigate, try and punish human rights violations. The few judges that kept their independence and did not relinquish the exercise of their tutelary functions were victims of repressive acts, including murder and threats, especially during the 1980s.

The CEH concludes that the rights to life and due process of those citizens that the Government of Guatemala put on trial in the Courts of Special Jurisdiction were also seriously violated, particularly in the numerous cases in which the death penalty was imposed.

During the entire period of the internal armed confrontation, the Guatemalan Army illegally forced thousands of young men into the army to participate directly in hostilities. Forced recruitment, which discriminated against the Mayan people and included minors under the age of fifteen, was a violation of personal freedom.

The Government Has Violated Human Rights Law

The CEH concludes that the events referred to herein are grave violations of international human rights law whose precepts the Guatemalan State has been committed to respect since it approved the Universal Declaration of Human Rights and the American Declaration of the Rights and Obligations of Man in 1948. The fundamental principles of human rights have achieved the category of international customary law.

The gravity of this conclusion is accentuated by the fact that some of these violations, especially arbitrary executions, forced disappearances and torture, were repeated throughout the entire internal armed confrontation, at some stages becoming systematic. This obliges the authorities of the Guatemalan State to accept historical responsibility for these violations before the Guatemalan people and the international community.

As regards international humanitarian law, which contains the obligatory rules for all armed conflicts (including non-international armed conflicts), the CEH concludes that Guatemalan State agents, the majority of whom were members of the Army, flagrantly committed acts prohibited by Common Article III of the 1949 Geneva Conventions, particularly with respect to attacks against life and bodily integrity, mutilation, cruel treatment, torture and torment, the taking of hostages, attacks on personal dignity, and particularly humiliating and degrading treatment, including the rape of women. Therefore, the State of Guatemala, which was legally obliged to comply with these precepts and prohibitions throughout the confrontation, is responsible for these infractions.

The CEH concludes that the State of Guatemala, especially its Army, failed to make the distinction that applies in all types of armed conflicts, between combatants and non-combatants, that is, between those who participate directly in hostilities resorting to arms for self-defence or for neutralising the enemy, and the civilian population that does not take part in hostilities, including those who previously participated, but no longer do so because they were wounded, became sick or laid down their arms.

Neither did the State of Guatemala respect the distinction between military targets and civilian property, proceeding to destroy, at great harm to the people, private and community property which, due to their nature, location, objective or use, were not military targets. Evidence of violations of these principles can be found in the multiple scorched earth operations and in registered cases of property destruction, as well as in the destruction of the collectively worked fields and harvests, which was a specific objective of the military plan, *Firmness 83-1.*

Moreover, the CEH concludes that the events presented in this report are grave violations of common principles that unite international human rights law and international humanitarian law. These principles were an historical demand of peoples who have faced unacceptable acts of barbarity during the twentieth century, events which never should be forgotten or repeated.

Finally, the CEH concludes that all these actions openly violate the rights guaranteed by the different constitutions of Guatemala in existence during the internal armed confrontation.

An Institutional Policy of Violating Human Rights

The majority of human rights violations occurred with the knowledge or by order of the highest authorities of the State. Evidence from different sources (declarations made by previous members of the armed forces, documentation, declassified documents, data from various organizations, testimonies of well-known Guatemalans) all coincide with the fact that the intelligence services of the Army, especially the G-2 and the Presidential General Staff (*Estado Mayor Presidential*), obtained information about all kinds of individuals and civic organisations, evaluated their behaviour in their respective fields of activity, prepared lists of those actions that were to be repressed for their supposedly subversive character and proceeded accordingly to capture, interrogate, torture, forcibly disappear or execute these individuals.

The responsibility for a large part of these violations, with respect to the chain of military command as well as the political and administrative responsibility, reaches the highest levels of the Army and successive governments.

The excuse that lower ranking Army commanders were acting with a wide margin of autonomy and decentralisation without orders from superiors, as a way of explaining that "excesses" and "errors" were committed, is an unsubstantiated argument according to the CEH's investigation. The notorious fact that no high-commander, officer or person in the mid-level command of the Army or state security forces was tried or convicted for violation of human rights during all these years reinforces the evidence that the majority of these violations were the result of an institutional policy, thereby ensuring impenetrable impunity, which persisted during the whole period investigated by the CEH.

The Crime of Genocide Is Proven

The legal framework adopted by the CEH to analyse the possibility that acts of genocide were committed in Guatemala during the internal armed confrontation is the Convention on the Prevention and Punishment of the Crime of Genocide, adopted by the United Nations General Assembly on 9 December 1948 and ratified by the Guatemalan State by Decree 704 on 30 November 1949.

Article II of this instrument defines the crime of genocide and its requirements in the following terms:

> . . . genocide means any of the following acts committed with intent to destroy, in whole or in part, a national, ethnical, racial or religious group, as such:
>
> a) Killing members of the group;
>
> b) Causing serious bodily or mental harm to members of the group;
>
> c) Deliberately inflicting on the group conditions of life calculated to bring about its physical destruction in whole or in part;
>
> d) Imposing measures intended to prevent births within the group;

e) Forcibly transferring children of the group to another group.

On this basis, the two fundamental elements of the crime are: intentionality and that the acts committed include at least one of the five previously cited in the above article.

Acceptance and Nobel Lecture

Rigoberta Menchú Tum

In her speech accepting the 1992 Nobel Peace Prize, Guatemalan activist Rigoberta Menchú Tum puts her award into the context of a five-hundred-year struggle for survival by her Mayan people. In the following viewpoint, she says the recognition brought by the prize should bring hope to her country as well as a positive response from other nations. In a time when peace in her own country is not yet assured, she invites all nations to join in celebrating the common thread of positive humanity. Rigoberta Menchú Tum is an indigenous K'iche' Guatemalan woman who became an activist and author.

Your Majesties, the King and Queen of Norway,
The Honorable Members of the Nobel Peace Committee
Your Excellency, the Prime Minister,
Your Exellencies, Members of the Government and the Diplomatic Corps,
Dear Guatemalan countrymen and women,
Ladies and Gentlemen,

I feel a deep emotion and pride for the honor of having been awarded the Nobel Peace Prize for 1992. A deep personal feeling and pride for my country and its very ancient culture. For the values of the community and the people to which I belong, for the love of my country, of Mother Nature. Whoever understands this respects life and encourages the struggle that aims at such objectives.

I consider this Prize, not as a reward to me personally, but rather as one of the greatest conquests in the struggle for peace, for Human Rights and for the rights of the indigenous people, who, for 500 years, have been split, fragmented, as well as the victims of genocides, repression and discrimination.

Please allow me to convey to you all, what this Prize means to me.

In my opinion, the Nobel Peace Prize calls upon us to act in accordance with what it represents, and the great significance it has worldwide. In addition to being a priceless treasure, it is an instrument with which to fight for peace, for justice, for the rights of those who suffer the abysmal economical, social, cultural and political inequalities, typical of the order of the world in which we live, and where the transformation into a new world based on the values of the human being, is the expectation of the majority of those who live on this planet.

This Nobel Prize represents a standard bearer that encourages us to continue denouncing the violation of Human Rights, committed against the people in Guatemala, in America and in the world, and to perform a positive role in respect of the pressing task in my country, which is to achieve peace with social justice.

The Nobel Prize is a symbol of peace, and of the efforts to build up a real democracy. It will stimulate the civil sectors so that through a solid national unity, these may contribute to the process of negotiations that seek peace, reflecting the general feeling—although at times not possible to express because of fear—of Guatemalan society: to establish political and legal grounds that will give irreversible impulses to a solution to what initiated the internal armed conflict.

There is no doubt whatsoever that it constitutes a sign of hope in the struggle of the indigenous people in the entire Continent.

It is also a tribute to the Central-American people who are still searching for their stability, for the structuring of their future, and the path for their development and integration, based on civil democracy and mutual respect.

The importance of this Nobel Prize has been demonstrated by all the congratulations received from everywhere, from Heads of Government—practically all the American Presidents—to the organizations of the indigenous people and of Human Rights, from all over the world. In fact, what they see in this Nobel Peace Prize is not only a reward and a recognition of a single person, but a starting point for the hard struggle towards the achievement of that revindication which is yet to be fulfilled.

As a contrast, and paradoxically, it was actually in my own country where I met, on the part of some people, the strongest objections, reserve and indifference, for the award of the Nobel Peace Prize to this Quiché Indian. Perhaps because in Latin America, it is precisely in Guatemala where the discrimination towards the indigenous, towards women, and the repression of the longing for justice and peace, are more deeply rooted in certain social and political sectors.

Under present circumstances, in this disordered and complex world, the decision of the Norwegian Nobel Peace Prize Committee to award this honorable distinction to me, reflects the awareness of the fact that, in this way, courage and strength is given to the struggle of peace, reconciliation and justice; to the struggle against racism, cultural discrimination, and hence contributes to the achievement of harmonious co-existence between our people.

With deep pain, on one side, but with satisfaction on the other, I have to inform you that the Nobel Peace Prize 1992 will have to remain temporarily in Mexico City, in watchful waiting for peace in Guatemala. Because there are no political conditions in my country that would indicate or make me foresee a prompt and just solution. The satisfaction and gratitude are due to the fact that Mexico, our brother neighbor country, that has been so dedicated and interested, that has made such great efforts in respect of the negotiations that are being conducted to achieve peace, that has received and admitted so many refugees and exiled Guatemalans, has given us a place in the Museo del Templo Mayor (the cradle of the ancient Aztecs) so that the Nobel Prize may remain there, until peaceful and safe conditions are established in Guatemala to place it here, in the land of the Quetzal.[1]

When evaluating the overall significance of the award of the Peace Prize, I would like to say some words on behalf of all those whose voice cannot be heard or who have been repressed for having spoken their opinions, of all those who have been marginalized, who have been discriminated, who live in poverty, in need, of all those who are the victims of repression and violation of human rights. Those who, nevertheless, have endured through centuries, who have not lost their conscience, determination, and hope.

Please allow me, ladies and gentlemen, to say some words about my country and the civilization of the Mayas. The Maya people developed and spread geographically through some 300,000 square km; they occupied parts of the South of Mexico, Belize, Guatemala, as well as Honduras and El Salvador; they developed a very rich civilization in the area of political organization, as well as in social and economic fields; they were great scientists in the fields of mathematics, astronomy, agriculture, architecture and engineering; they were great artists in the fields of sculpture, painting, weaving and carving.

The Mayas discovered the zero value in mathematics, at about the same time that it was discovered in India and later passed on to the Arabs. Their astronomic forecasts based on mathematical calculations and scientific observations were amazing, and still are. They prepared a calendar more accurate than the Gregorian, and in the field of medicine they performed intracranial surgical operations.

One of the Maya books, which escaped destruction by the conquistadores, known as *The Codex of Dresden*, contains the results of an investigation on eclipses as well a table of 69 dates, in which solar eclipse occur in a lapse of 33 years.

Today, it is important to emphasize the deep respect that the Maya civilization had towards life and nature in general.

Who can predict what other great scientific conquests and developments these people could have achieved, if they had not been conquered by blood and fire, and subjected to an ethnocide that affected nearly 50 million people in the course of 500 years.

I would describe the meaning of this Nobel Peace prize, in the first place as a tribute to the Indian people who have been sacrificed and have disappeared because they aimed at a more dignified and just life with fraternity and understanding among human beings. To those who are no longer alive to keep up the hope for a change in the situation in respect of poverty and marginalization of the Indians, of those who have been banished, of the helpless in Guatemala as well as in the entire American Continent.

This growing concern is comforting, even though it comes 500 years later, to the suffering, the discrimination, the oppression and the exploitation that our peoples have been exposed to, but who, thanks to their own cosmovision—and concept of life, have managed to withstand and finally see some promising prospects. How those roots, that were to be eradicated, now begin to grow with strength, hope and visions of the future!

It also represents a sign of the growing international interest for, and understanding of the original Rights of the People, of the future of more than 60 million Indians that live in our Americas, and their outcry because of the 500 years of oppression that they have endured. For the genocide beyond comparison that they have had to suffer throughout this epoch, and from which other countries and the elite of the Americas have profited and taken advantage.

Let there be freedom for the Indians, wherever they may be in the American Continent or elsewhere in the world, because

A Mayan Survivor Gained World Attention for Her Cause

Rigoberta Menchú Tum (1959–) became Guatemala's most famous woman when she won the Nobel Peace Prize in 1992. As an activist and organizer, she highlighted the injustices against indigenous people, women in particular. She did so in dangerous circumstances. Guatemalan armed forces killed her mother, father, brother, and other family members during the campaign against native-born Mayans in the country. The campaign was later declared to be genocide.

Menchú, who at age thirteen worked as a maid to a rich family in Guatemala City, pursued an education and became active in several anti-government human rights groups. In 1981 she fled to safety in Mexico and continued her efforts from there, returning to Guatemala when it became more peaceful.

In her 1983 autobiography, *I, Rigoberta Menchú*, published when she was twenty-three, she details an arduous childhood in a poor peasant family. A later book by US anthropology professor David Stoll revealed substantial factual discrepancies in Menchú's account, including that her family was wealthier than she claimed. She eventually admitted she portrayed herself as more impoverished to gain sympathy for her cause.

while they are alive, a glow of hope will be alive as well as a true concept of life.

The expressions of great happiness by the Indian Organizations in the entire Continent and the worldwide congratulations received for the award of the Nobel Peace Prize, clearly indicate the great importance of this decision. It is the recognition of the European debt to the American indigenous people; it is an appeal to the conscience of Humanity so that those conditions of marginalization that condemned them to colonialism and exploitation may be eradicated; it is a cry for life, peace, justice, equality and fraternity between human beings.

The peculiarities of the vision of the Indian people are expressed according to the way in which they are related to each other. First, between human beings, through communication. Second, with the earth, as with our mother, because she gives us our lives and is not mere merchandise. Third, with nature, because we are an integral part of it, and not its owners.

To us Mother Earth is not only a source of economic riches that give us the maize, which is our life, but she also provides so many other things that the privileged ones of today strive for. The Earth is the root and the source of our culture. She keeps our memories, she receives our ancestors and she, therefore, demands that we honor her and return to her, with tenderness and respect, those goods that she gives us. We have to take care of her so that our children and grandchildren may continue to benefit from her. If the world does not learn now to show respect to nature, what kind of future will the new generations have?

From these basic features derive behavior, rights and obligations in the American Continent, for the indigenous people as well as for the non-indigenous, whether they be racially mixed, blacks, whites or Asian. The whole society has an obligation to show mutual respect, to learn from each other and to share material and scientific achievements, in the most convenient way. The indigenous peoples never had, and still do not have, the place that they should have occupied in the progress and benefits of science and technology, although they represented an important basis for this development.

If the indigenous civilization and the European civilizations could have made exchanges in a peaceful and harmonious manner, without destruction, exploitation, discrimination and poverty, they could, no doubt, have achieved greater and more valuable conquests for Humanity.

Let us not forget that when the Europeans came to America, there was flourishing and strong civilization there. One cannot talk about a "discovery of America", because one discovers that which one does not known about, or that which is hidden. But

America and its native civilizations had discovered themselves long before the fall of the Roman Empire and Medieval Europe. The significance of its cultures forms part of the heritage of humanity and continues to astonish the learned.

I think it is necessary that the indigenous peoples, of which I am a member, should contribute their science and knowledge to human development, because we have enormous potential and we could combine our very ancient heritage with the achievements of European civilization as well as with civilizations in other parts of the world.

But this contribution, that to our understanding is a recovery of the natural and cultural heritage, must take place based on a rational and consensual basis in respect of the right to make use of knowledge and natural resources, with guarantees for equality between Government and society.

We the indigenous are willing to combine tradition with modernism, but not at any cost. We will not tolerate or permit that our future be planned as possible guardians of ethno-touristic projects on a continental level.

At a time when the commemoration of the Fifth Centenary of the arrival of Columbus in America has repercussions all over the world, the revival of hope for the oppressed indigenous peoples demands that we reassert our existence to the world and the value of our cultural identity. It demands that we endeavor to actively participate in the decisions that concern our destiny, in the building-up of our countries/nations. Should we, in spite of all, not be taken into consideration, there are factors that guarantee our future: struggle and endurance; courage; the decision to maintain our traditions that have been exposed to so many perils and sufferings; solidarity towards our struggle on the part of numerous countries, governments, organizations and citizens of the world.

That is why I dream of the day when the relationship between the indigenous peoples and other peoples is strengthened; when they can combine their potentialities and their capabilities and contribute to make life on this planet less unequal, a better distribution of the scientific and cultural treasures accumulated by Humanity, flourishing in peace and justice.

Today, in the 47th period of sessions of the General Assembly, the United nations (UN) will proclaim 1993 as the *International Year of the World's Indigenous People*, in the presence of well-known chiefs of the organizations of the Indian people and of the coordination of the Continental Movement of Indigenous, Blacks and Popular Resistance. They will all formally participate in the opening of the working sessions in order to make 1993 a year of specific actions to truly place the indigenous peoples within their national contexts and to make them part of mutual international agreements.

The achievement of the *International Year of the World's Indigenous People* and the progress represented by the preparation of the project for the *Universal Declaration*, are the result of the participation of numerous Indian brothers, nongovernmental organizations and the successful efforts of the experts in the Working group, in addition to the comprehensiveness shown by many countries in the United Nations.

We hope that the formulation of the project in respect of the Declaration on the Rights of the indigenous People will examine and go deeply into the existing difficult reality that we, the Indo-Americans, experience.[2]

Our people will have a year dedicated to the problems that afflict them and, in this respect, are now getting ready to carry out different activities with the purpose of presenting proposals and putting pressure on action plans. All this will be conducted in the most reasonable way and with the most convincing and justified arguments for the elimination of racism, oppression, discrimination and the exploitation of those who have been dragged into poverty and oblivion. Also for "the condemned of the earth", the award of the Nobel Peace Prize represents a recognition, an encouragement and an objective for the future.

I wish that a conscious sense of peace and a feeling of human solidarity would develop in all peoples, which would open new relationships of respect and equality for the next millennium, to be ruled by fraternity and not by cruel conflicts.

Opinion is being formed everywhere today, that in spite of wars and violence, calls upon the entire human race to protect its historical values and to form unity in diversity. And this calls upon us all to reflect upon the incorporation of important elements of change and transformation in all aspects of life on earth, in the search for specific and definite solutions to the deep ethical crisis that afflicts Humanity. This will, no doubt have decisive influence on the structure of the future.

There is a possibility that some centers of political and economic power, some statesmen and intellectuals, have not yet managed to see the advantages of the active participation of the indigenous peoples in all the fields of human activity. However, the movement initiated by different political and intellectual "Amerindians" will finally convince them that, from an objective point of view, we are a constituent part of the historical alternatives that are being discussed at the international level.

Ladies and gentlemen, allow me to say some candid words about my country.

The attention that this Nobel Peace Prize has focused on Guatemala should imply that the violation of the human rights is no longer ignored internationally. It will also honor all those who died in the struggle for social equality and justice in my country.

It is known throughout the world that the Guatemalan people, as a result of their struggle, succeeded in achieving, in October 1944, a period of democracy where institutionality and human rights were the main philosophies. At that time, Guatemala was an exception in the American Continent, because of its struggle for complete national sovereignty. However, in 1954, a conspiracy that associated the traditional national power centers, inheritors of colonialism, with powerful foreign interests, overthrew the democratic regime as a result of an armed invasion, thereby re-imposing the old system of oppression which has characterized the history of my country.[3]

The economic, social and political subjection that derived from the Cold War, was what initiated the internal armed conflict. The repression against the organizations of the people, the democratic parties and the intellectuals, started in Guatemala long before the war started. Let us not forget that.

In the attempt to crush rebellion, dictatorships have committed the greatest atrocities. They have leveled villages, and murdered thousands of peasants particularly Indians, hundreds of trade union workers and students, outstanding intellectuals and politicians, priests and nuns. Through this systematic persecution in the name of the safety of the nation, one million peasants were removed by force from their lands; 100,000 had to seek refuge in the neighboring countries. In Guatemala, there are today almost 100,000 orphans and more than 40,000 widows. The practice of "disappeared" politicians was invented in Guatemala, as a government policy.

As you know, I am myself a survivor of a massacred family.

The country collapsed into a crisis never seen before and the changes in the world forced and encouraged the military forces to permit a political opening that consisted in the preparation of a new Constitution, in an expansion of the political field, and in the transfer of the government to civil sectors. We have had this new regime for eight years and in certain fields there have been some openings of importance.

However, in spite of these openings, repression and violation of human rights persists in the middle of an economic crisis, that is becoming more and more acute, to the extent that 84% of the population is today considered as poor, and some 60% are considered as very poor. Impunity and terror continue to prevent people from freely expressing their needs and vital demands. The internal armed conflict still exists.

The political life in my country has lately centered around the search for a political solution to the global crisis and the armed conflict that has existed in Guatemala since 1962. This process was initiated by the Agreement signed in this City of

Oslo, between the Comisión Nacional de Reconciliación with government mandate, and the Unidad Revolucionaria Nacional Guatemalteca (URNG) as a necessary step to introduce to Guatemala the spirit of the Agreement of Esquipulas.[4]

As a result of this Agreement and conversations between the URNG and different sectors of Guatemalan society, direct negotiations were initiated under the government of President Serrano, between the government and the guerrillas, as a result of which three agreements have already been signed. However, the subject of Human Rights has taken a long time, because this subject constitutes the core of the Guatemalan problems, and around this core important differences have arisen. Nevertheless, there has been considerable progress.

The process of negotiations aims at reaching agreements in order to establish the basis for a real democracy in Guatemala and for an end to the war. As far as I understand, with the good-will of the parties concerned and the active participation of the civil sectors, adapting to a great national unity, the phase of purposes and intentions could be left behind so that Guatemala could be pulled out of the crossroads that seem to have become eternal.

Dialogues and political negotiations are, no doubt, adequate means to solve these problems, in order to respond in a specific way to the vital and urgent needs for life and for the implementation of democracy for the Guatemalan people. However, I am convinced that if the diverse social sectors which integrate Guatemalan society find bases of unity, respecting their natural differences, they would together find a solution to those problems and therefore resolve the causes which initiated the war which prevails in Guatemala.

Other civil sectors as well as the international community must demand that the negotiations between the Government and the URNG surpass the period in which they are finding themselves in discussing Human Rights and move ahead as soon as possible to a verifiable agreement with the United Nations. It

Rigoberta Menchú Tum participates in a 2012 ceremony to mark the thirty-second anniversary of the attack on the Spanish embassy in Guatemala City. Thirty-seven people were killed during the attack, including Menchú's father. © AP Images/Moises Castillo.

is necessary to point out, here in Oslo, that the issue of Human Rights in Guatemala constitutes, at present, the most urgent problem that has to be solved. My statement is neither incidental nor unjustified.

As has been ascertained by international institutions, such as The United Nations Commission on Human Rights, The Interamerican Commission of Human Rights and many other humanitarian organizations, Guatemala is one of the countries in America with the largest number of violations of these rights, and the largest number of cases of impunity where security forces are generally involved. It is imperative that the repression and persecution of the people and the Indians be stopped. The compulsory mobilization and integration of young people into the Patrols of Civil Self Defense, which principally affects the Indian people, must also be stopped.

Democracy in Guatemala must be built-up as soon as possible. It is necessary that Human Rights agreements be fully complied with, i.e. an end to racism; guaranteed freedom to organize and to move within all sectors of the country. In short, it is imperative to open all fields to the multi-ethnic civil society with all its rights, to demilitarize the country and establish the basis for its development, so that it can be pulled out of today's underdevelopment and poverty.

Among the most bitter dramas that a great percentage of the population has to endure, is the forced exodus. Which means, to be forced by military units and persecution to abandon their villages, their Mother Earth, where their ancestors rest, their environment, the nature that gave them life and the growth of their communities, all of which constituted a coherent system of social organization and functional democracy.

The case of the displaced and of refugees in Guatemala is heartbreaking; some of them are condemned to live in exile in other countries, but the great majority live in exile in their own country. They are forced to wander from place to place, to live in ravines and inhospitable places, some not recognized as

Guatemalan citizens, but all of them are condemned to poverty and hunger. There cannot be a true democracy as long as this problem is not satisfactorily solved and these people are reinstated on their lands and in their villages.

In the new Guatemalan society, there must be a fundamental reorganization in the matter of land ownership, to allow for the development of the agricultural potential, as well as for the return of the land to the legitimate owners. This process of reorganization must be carried out with the greatest respect for nature, in order to protect her and return to her, her strength and capability to generate life.

No less characteristic of a democracy is social justice. This demands a solution to the frightening statistics on infant mortality, of malnutrition, lack of education, analphabetism, wages insufficient to sustain life. These problems have a growing and painful impact on the Guatemalan population and imply no prospects and no hope.

Among the features that characterize society today, is that of the role of women, although female emancipation has not, in fact, been fully achieved so far by any country in the world.

The historical development in Guatemala reflects now the need and the irreversibility of the active contribution of women to the configuration of the new Guatemalan social order, of which, I humbly believe, the Indian women already are a clear testimony. This Nobel Peace Prize is a recognition to those who have been, and still are in most parts of the world, the most exploited of the exploited; the most discriminated of the discriminated, the most marginalized of the marginalized, but still those who produce life and riches.

Democracy, development and modernization of a country are impossible and incongruous without the solution of these problems.

In Guatemala, it is just as important to recognize the Identity and the Rights of the Indigenous Peoples, that have been ignored and despised not only during the colonial period, but also during the Republic. It is not possible to conceive a democratic Guatemala, free and independent, without the indigenous identity shaping its character into all aspects of national existence.

It will undoubtedly be something new, a completely new experience, with features that, at the moment, we cannot describe. But it will authentically respond to history and the characteristics of the real Guatemalan nationality. The true profile that has been distorted for such a long time.

This urgency of this vital need, are the issues that urge me, at this moment, from this rostrum, to urge national opinion and the international community, to show a more active interest in Guatemala.

Taking into consideration that in connection with my role as a Nobel Prize Winner, in the process of negotiations for peace in Guatemala many possibilities have been handled, but now I think that this role is more likely to be the role of a promoter of peace, of national unity, for the protection of the rights of the indigenous peoples. In such a way, that I may take initiatives in accordance with the needs, and thereby prevent the Peace Prize from becoming a piece of paper that has been pigeonholed.

I call upon all the social and ethnic sectors that constitute the people of Guatemala to participate actively in the efforts to find a peaceful solution to the armed conflict, to build-up a sound unity between the "ladinos,"[5] the blacks and the Indians, all of whom must create within their diverse groups, a "Guatemality".

Along these same lines, I invite the international community to contribute with specific actions so that the parties involved may overcome the differences that at this stage keep negotiations in a wait-and-see state, so that they will succeed, first of all, in signing an agreement on Human Rights. And then, to re-initiate the rounds of negotiation and identify those issues on which to compromise, to allow for the Peace Agreement to be signed and immediately ratified, because I have no doubt that this will bring about great relief in the prevailing situation in Guatemala.

My opinion is also that the UN should have a more direct participation, which would go further than playing the role of observer, and could help substantially to move the process ahead.

Ladies and gentlemen, the fact that I have given preference to the American Continent, and in particular to my country, does not mean that I do not have an important place in my mind and in my heart for the concern of other peoples of the world and their constant struggle in the defense of peace, of the right to a life and all its inalienable rights. The majority of us who are gathered here today, constitute an example of the above, and along these lines I would humbly extend to you my gratitude.

Many things have changed in these last years. There have been great changes of worldwide character. The East-West confrontation has ceased to exist and the Cold War has come to an end. These changes, the exact forms of which cannot yet be predicted, have left gaps that the people of the world have known how to make use of in order to come forward, struggle and win national terrain and international recognition.

Today, we must fight for a better world, without poverty, without racism, with peace in the Middle East and in Southeast Asia, to where I address a plea for the liberation of Mrs. Aung San Suu Kyi, winner of the Nobel Peace Prize 1991; for a just and peaceful solution, in the Balkans; for the end of the apartheid in South Africa; for the stability in Nicaragua, that the Peace Agreement in El Salvador be observed; for the re-establishment of democracy in Haiti; for the complete sovereignty of Panama; because all of these constitute the highest aims for justice in the international situation.

A world at peace that could provide consistency, interrelations and concordance in respect of the economic, social and cultural structures of the societies would indeed have deep roots and a robust influence.

We have in our mind the deepest felt demands of the entire human race, when we strive for peaceful co-existence and the preservation of the environment. The struggle we fight purifies and shapes the future.

Our history is a living history that has throbbed, withstood and survived many centuries of sacrifice. Now it comes forward again with strength. The seeds, dormant for such a long time, break out today with some uncertainty, although they germinate in a world that is at present characterized by confusion and uncertainty.

There is no doubt that this process will be long and complex, but it is no Utopia and we, the Indians, we have new confidence in its implementation.

The peoples of Guatemala will mobilize and will be aware of their strength in building up a worthy future. They are preparing themselves to sow the future, to free themselves from atavisms, to rediscover their heritage. To build a country with a genuine national identity. To start a new life.

By combining all the shades and nuances of the "ladinos", the "garífunas"[6] and Indians in the Guatemalan ethnic mosaic, we must interlace a number of colors without introducing contradictions, without becoming grotesque nor antagonistic, but we must give them brightness and a superior quality, just the way our weavers weave a typical huipil blouse, brilliantly composed, a gift to Humanity.

Thank you very much.

Notes

1. The government and the guerrillas signed a peace agreement in December 1996, but Rigoberta's Nobel medal and diploma still remain at the Museo del Templo Mayor in Mexico City.
   The quetzal is the national bird of Guatemala.
2. The reference is to the Declaration on Rights of Persons Belonging to National, Ethnic, Religious and Linguistic Minorities, which was adopted by the General Assembly of the United Nations on December 18, 1992. The Working Group was the Working Group on Indigenous Populations of the Subcommission on Prevention of Discrimination and Protection of Minorities.

3. The revolution of 1944 brought to power the presidential regime of Dr. Juan José Arévalo, who instituted democratic and social reforms. His successor, Jacobo Arbenz Guzmán, was considered to be pro-communists by the government of President Dwight D. Eisenhower of the United States, which ordered the CIA to cooperate with right-wing and military forces in an armed invasion which overthrew the Arbenz government in 1954. The ensuing period of repression led to the civil war which lasted from 1962 to 1996.

4. This agreement between the governmental National Commission for Reconciliation and the guerrilla Guatemalan National Revolutionary Unity was signed at Oslo in March 1990. It was a further step in the efforts of the two Guatemalan parties to end their armed conflict, a process in which the government of Guatemala was participating along with El Salvador, Honduras, Costa Rica and Nicaragua. The five presidents had made several attempts to agree on measures to end the civil wars in Central American countries, one of their summits having taken place in Esquipulas, Guatemala, in 1986. President Oscar Arias Sánchez of Costa Rica took a leading role in these negotiations, which were finally successful in the multilateral agreement signed in August 1987. For his contribution Arias received the Nobel Peace prize that year. See the previous volume in this series, Nobel Lectures. Peace, 1981–1990, pp. 181–182.

5. The ladinos are of Spanish and Indian descent.

6. The garifunas are a tiny ethnic group on the Atlantic coast, of African-Carib descent.

CHAPTER 2

Controversies Surrounding the Repression in El Salvador and Guatemala

Chapter Exercises

As peace was established in Guatemala and El Salvador, their national budgets diverged on what areas their governments thought were most important. The examples below are in budget percentages.

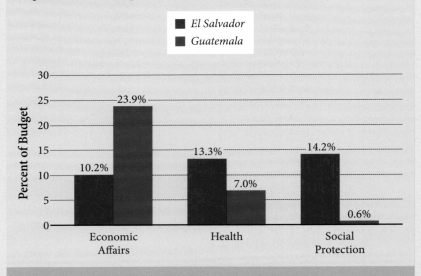

Source: International Monetary Fund, *Government Finance Statistics Yearbook*, 2003.

1. Analyze the Chart

Question 1: Judging by what you see in the chart, business people have more influence in which of the two countries?

Question 2: Based on the chart, which country leans more toward liberal policies?

Question 3: Does the chart say that Salvadorans are almost twice as healthy as Guatemalans? Please give a brief explanation along with your answer.

2. Writing Prompt:

Choose one of the photographs in this chapter, imagine you are a person in the photograph, and write approximately one page about your life.

3. Group Activity:

Divide into four groups. Assume the year is 1990. One group represents the right-wing leadership of El Salvador, one is the rebel coalition in El Salvador, one is the right-wing leadership of Guatemala, and one represents the Mayan guerrillas in Guatemala. Based on readings in this chapter, each group should present a list of three justifications for its actions.

Strategy Choices by Both Sides Led to a Salvadoran Stalemate

Hugh Byrne

In the following viewpoint, a policy analyst contends that through-out the Salvadoran civil war, the insurgents' strategy enabled them to survive against government forces, but did not generate enough support to overthrow the government. Yet, he argues, the govern-ment's strategy of containment failed to put the guerrillas out of business. The result was a bloody and costly stalemate, according to the author, who based his analysis on twelve thousand previ-ously secret US documents, files of the insurgents, and interviews with leading participants in the conflict. Hugh Byrne, a consultant to non-governmental organizations concerned with US policy in Latin America, spent 1987–1991 in Washington, D.C., as politi-cal director of the Committee in Solidarity with the People of El Salvador.

S trategy was an important factor in the outcome of the eleven-year Salvadoran civil war, but in a negative more than a posi-tive sense. The insurgents were able to *neutralize* all efforts by the counterrevolutionary coalition to marginalize and defeat them, but were not able to expand their base of support and gen-

Hugh Byrne, "Conclusion," *El Salvador's Civil War: A Study of Revolution.* Boulder, CO: Lynne Rienner Publishers, 1996, pp. 201–207. Copyright © 1996 by Lynne Rienner Publishers, Inc. Used with permission by the publisher.

erate a violent insurrection to overthrow the government. The Salvadoran government and military and their U.S. backers were able to *contain* the FMLN [Farabundo Martí National Liberation Front, a guerrilla group] militarily and politically so as to ensure that a military offensive and popular insurrection did not succeed but were unable to isolate and defeat the rebels as their strategies had promised. The ultimate political outcome reflected this mutual veto.

The FMLN brought to the conflict a single-minded commitment to winning power through a political-military strategy of revolutionary war. This involved unifying political, military, economic, diplomatic, and other initiatives to defeat the Salvadoran government and armed forces. This grand strategy took different forms in different periods. From 1981 to 1984, military objectives predominated. Thus, while the groundwork was laid for a prolonged guerrilla war, the efforts to win a speedy military victory played to some of the strengths of the government side and limited the reach and effectiveness of the FMLN as a political force.

In the next period, a major shift in rebel grand strategy caused some short-term weaknesses but helped create the conditions for a prolonged war leading to a strategic counteroffensive to overthrow the government. During this period, rebel efforts on a variety of levels were articulated to contribute to the goal of weakening the government politically, and wearing out the military in a war of attrition in preparation for the counteroffensive. This strategy culminated in the November 1989 offensive that demonstrated to major Salvadoran and U.S. actors the failure of their ambitious political and military strategies to defeat the insurgents.

In the final period of the war, late 1989 to late 1991, the FMLN's grand strategy focused on political negotiations as the optimal and most probable means of resolving the conflict. There were differences within and among the parties in the FMLN as to the possibility of winning a favorable solution through negotiations, and on the relative importance of military and negotiating strategies. Moreover, military actions continued to play an important role in increasing pressure to win concessions at the bargaining table. Nevertheless, throughout this period the impact of the FMLN's earlier strategies and the changed international and Salvadoran environments placed negotiations at the center of the insurgents' grand strategy.

Gaps Persisted Between Plans and Actions

For most of the eleven years of the civil war, the United States and its Salvadoran allies either lacked a grand strategy for defeating the insurgents or held the strategy in theory but failed to implement it in practice. Between 1981 and 1984 the counterrevolutionary coalition affected major strategic initiatives to stabilize the economy, legitimate the government domestically and internationally through elections, and turn around the military situation through extensive military aid and advice. But these efforts were largely piecemeal and uncoordinated.

In the next period, from mid-1984 to the 1989 FMLN offensive, the United States and its allies developed a grand strategy to defeat the insurgents through waging a low-intensity war to win political support for the government and armed forces, and to isolate and erode the guerrillas as a political-military force. This strategy involved a sophisticated counterinsurgency effort to win the sympathy of the population through civic-action programs, psychological-warfare campaigns, and the creation of civil-defense units. These efforts were to be supported by a quantitative and qualitative improvement of the military, institutional changes to increase the legitimacy of the government, and major efforts to rebuild the economy. In practice, however, they fell victim to divisions among the major components of the counterinsurgency coalition, PDC government [the Christian Democratic Party] incompetence and corruption, the military's unwillingness to change, and FMLN strategies designed to weaken the government politically and the armed forces militarily. In the final years of the war, 1989 to 1991, the United States and its allies came closest to implementing a unified strategy to achieve their objectives. But by this stage, the effort was largely defensive in nature and intended to ensure that the government and armed forces remained intact and did not have to concede too much in the process of negotiations.

The problem of strategy for the counterrevolutionary coalition lay in the nature of the coalition itself and can be traced to the U.S. decision to become deeply involved in the Salvadoran conflict in late 1979 and early 1980. At that stage, key decisions were made that would have implications throughout the war. The primary objective was defined as defeating the armed insurgency. To undercut the appeal of the revolutionaries, actions were taken to weaken the domination of the traditional oligarchy, particularly through the agrarian reform and nationalization of the banks and foreign trade. But, for fear of weakening the opposition to the insurgency, the most important part of the land reform was shelved indefinitely, and the oligarchy, though dislocated, was not broken as an economic or political force. This ensured that the traditional landowning class and its political representatives remained a potent political force that worked continuously to undermine the reforms and win back political power. It also guaranteed that the reforms, which might have had a greater impact in weakening the insurgency if they had been fully implemented, were more significant on a level of public relations than in "taking the revolution from the revolutionaries."

The U.S. Effort Was Unrealistic

Similarly, the U.S. government cast its lot with conservative military officers who were known by U.S. intelligence agencies to be involved in massacres and death-squad activities and who, by late 1980, had wrested control of the institution from progressive officers. This decision was made to ensure that the primary objective of defeating the insurgents was not compromised; the result was a constant struggle on the part of U.S. political and military

Hoping to gain support for their cause, rebel leaders explain their motives to a crowd in Berlin, El Salvador, in 1983. Two boys hold a rebel flag in the background. © Bettmann/Corbis.

officials to change the attitudes and practices of military leaders while claiming to Congress and the American people that the armed forces had been transformed decisively. Throughout the 1980s the Salvadoran military paid lip service to human rights and civilian control while continuing to violate human rights and prevent the punishment of its members for murders and other serious crimes. Having made the decision to work with and through the leadership of the Salvadoran armed forces and to attempt to bring the Salvadoran oligarchy to participate constructively in the counterinsurgency war against the FMLN, the United States was in the position of trying to square the circle. It sought to win the hearts and minds of actual or potential rebel supporters through radical measures that would transform social relations, particularly in the Salvadoran countryside. However, it balked at taking the measures that might in practice have won support away from the insurgents, for fear of further dividing the counterrevolutionary coalition. Thus, symbolic actions and public-relations measures replaced the truly radical measures that counterinsurgency strategists have argued are necessary to defeat an entrenched insurgency. A military force that was notorious for carrying out massacres in the early 1980s was presenting itself a few years later as the defender of democracy and the protector of the people. Not surprisingly, there is scant evidence of this change winning many hearts and minds among the rural population.

Another major difference between the two sides lay in their levels of unity, which had a major impact on the effectiveness of the strategies implemented. The FMLN was made up of five political parties that each maintained its own structure, organization, finances, and leadership. The parties often had deep disagreements over strategy (e.g., the approach to negotiations in the early 1980s) and tactics (e.g., the appropriateness of kidnapping and killing mayors and local officials). But throughout the eleven years of war they maintained a central leadership that was responsible for the conduct of the war, and a unified approach to strategy that obliged all five parties to implement directives of the General Command (even if, at times, the level of enthusiasm varied). By contrast, the counterrevolutionary coalition never achieved strategic unity, and different political, economic, and institutional interests among the economic elite, the PDC, the military, and the United States prevented the implementation of a unified political-military strategy to win the war. The far right worked to undermine the political and economic initiatives of the PDC government in the mid-to-late 1980s. The armed forces sought to protect their own interests and to take the leading role in counterinsurgency to distance themselves from an unpopular government in the same period. The United States worked covertly to prevent right-wing electoral victories in 1982 and 1984, and sought to advance its own geostrategic interests in the country and the region. The contrasting levels of unity of the two sides made a difference to the effectiveness of each, and particularly to their ability to conceive and implement strategies that would advance their overall objectives.

Ultimately, the large disparity in access to political, military, and economic resources between the two sides was equalized by the advantages possessed by the FMLN in maintaining a unified front with an overall strategic vision. This was implemented in practice over a counterrevolutionary coalition that was deeply divided and unable to implement a shared vision of how to defeat the insurgency. In the terms of insurgency and counterinsurgency theory, the FMLN "won by not losing": By avoiding defeat, and having the potential to sustain the war into the future and prevent economic and social recovery, the insurgents ensured that peace would not be attained until many of their demands were achieved at the bargaining table. By the same token, however, the FMLN "lost by not winning": By failing to achieve the overthrow of the government through their political-military strategies, the insurgents had to accept at the culmination of negotiations the continued existence of the government and military that they had tried hard to oust. Instead of winning power, which was the rebels' central objective, they won the right to compete for power in a democratic setting. Because this had traditionally been denied to opposition elements and was a major cause of the war, it could be claimed as a victory. The price paid by the people and the society to reach this stalemate after eleven years of war was enormous.

Each Strategy Carried Large Costs

No specific strategies were decisive in ensuring the ultimate outcome of the Salvadoran conflict. What was more significant was the difference in the ability of the two sides to unify different approaches within a grand strategy to achieve their overall objectives. Certain strategies, however, were effective in strengthening the position of one side and weakening its opponent. For the FMLN the most effective strategies were those that prevented the government from implementing its own strategies for winning the sympathy of the civilian population, isolating the insurgents, and generating economic recovery. But the most effective strategies were also double-edged swords that carried with them political as well as human costs.

Sabotage helped prevent economic stabilization and recovery but also affected the lives and living standards of many, including the poor to whom the FMLN looked for support. The continuous destruction of electrical towers and posts, bridges, buses, and other forms of transportation undoubtedly had political costs, particularly among those not clearly aligned with either protagonist, and allowed the government to portray the rebels as a purely destructive force.

The war of attrition—particularly the use of land mines to kill and wound the maximum number of Salvadoran soldiers from the second half of the 1980s—lessened the speed and determination of Salvadoran military offensives, wore down military morale, and made the implementation of the war more difficult for the government. But it also killed and maimed many civilians (as well as soldiers) and allowed the government and the United States to present the FMLN as terrorists who were indifferent to the suffering they were causing.

The expansion of the war throughout the country and particularly to the capital, San Salvador, allowed the FMLN to present itself as a ubiquitous force that the government could not defeat, and helped convince U.S. policymakers responsible for funding the war that the decade-long counterinsurgency was not a success. But the actions carried out or encouraged by the FMLN in attempting to "unleash the violence of the masses"—car bombings, assassinations, and violent demonstrations—appear to have alienated many of those targeted by the rebels to support an insurrection.

The strategies of the U.S. and Salvadoran governments had immense human costs and were largely ineffective in weakening or defeating the insurgents. Military massacres and death-squad killings, organized by military officers and right-wing civilian allies, were not successful in defeating the FMLN but had great political costs that placed major constraints on the ability of the two governments to win financial and political support for the war. The major counterinsurgency campaigns sought to clear civilian supporters of the rebels from insurgent-dominated areas by aerial bombardment, army sweeps, or forced displacement, but they were not effective in undercutting the FMLN and had serious political costs because of the human-rights violations involved.

For the United States and its Salvadoran allies the most effective strategy adopted was the use of elections to legitimate the government and isolate the insurgents. The electoral strategy helped move the government from a position of domestic and international isolation to one in which it enjoyed greater domestic support (for a period) along with greater international legitimacy and recognition. The elections helped bring about a change in Salvadoran politics and society whereby sectors of the population not strongly identified with either the government or the FMLN held out some hope that voting in elections would help resolve their fundamental problems. However limited was this change, it appears to have been sufficient to persuade a proportion of the population to work within the electoral system rather than pin their hopes on a successful insurrection. The failure of the FMLN to spark a popular insurrection in November 1989 appears to be related to these changes that had taken place in Salvadoran society through the 1980s.

At the same time, there were limitations to the success of the electoral strategy in the absence of electoral outcomes that could help consolidate the disparate counterrevolutionary forces behind a unified strategy for defeating the FMLN. In practice, the electoral strategy did not succeed in weakening the FMLN substantially and, in spite of the institutionalization of a limited process of democratization, the rebels were able to maintain their core of popular support and wage a political-military campaign to weaken the government and military.

El Salvador's Military Operated Like Organized Crime

William Stanley

In the following viewpoint, a political science professor contends that El Salvador's military held power for decades by protecting elite citizens. The military could kill, steal from, and suppress large segments of the population as long as it allowed the members of the economic elite to retain their position and wealth, he argues. However, the author notes, this arrangement created an enemy the military could not defeat—a persistent guerrilla force. William Stanley teaches political science at the University of New Mexico, where he has served as director of Latin American studies.

How can we account for mass murder by the Salvadoran state? Most readers will find it difficult to conceive of the mentality and spirit that enable individual soldiers to torture, slaughter, and mutilate defenseless civilians, whatever the ideological justification. Viewing the violence analytically, as collective behavior, it seems difficult to escape the conclusion that it was irrational. Though state terrorism clearly intimidated and suppressed some kinds of opposition at some points along the way, it just as clearly motivated many people to raise arms against the state, filling them with grim determination to take revenge. As David Mason and Dale Krane have shown, when state violence becomes sufficiently intense and random, it becomes entirely rational for individuals to take arms to defend themselves. The state can create its own enemies, and by late 1983, the government of El Salvador had created so many that it faced serious risk of military defeat. Only massive U.S. assistance allowed the Armed Forces of El Salvador (FAES) to turn the tide and achieve a stalemate against the FMLN [Farabundo Martí National Liberation Front, a guerrilla group].

The conventional view in the social sciences is that state violence is a rational response to opposition. When social demands upon the state exceed the state's resources, or when opposition takes the form of violence and begins to threaten the state's control of society, then the state will logically respond with violence. This view has much in common with "realist" theories of international relations that focus on how and when states use force against one another: the challenge for the state lies in correctly calibrating its preparations for and use of violence to deter its enemies without goading them into making even more dangerous threats. By analogy to international relations theory, the domestic security dilemma facing the state is that failure to respond adequately to a threat may encourage its enemies; yet overreaction may produce more numerous and more radicalized internal enemies in the future.

This analysis certainly fits well with some aspects of violence in El Salvador. State violence clearly increased in response to greater popular opposition. Moreover, it appears that in some ways, repression had the effect of deterring social opposition: when the opposition FMLN tried to trigger a mass insurrection in January 1981, after more than a year of intense state terror, they found that most of the urban population was too frightened to take part. Yet, just as clearly, state violence had the effect of intensifying opposition to the state in many rural areas, generating a popular base for the FMLN guerrillas, which kept them supplied with food, shelter, intelligence, and recruits, resources that, combined with international assistance from various sources, enabled them to fight the FAES to a draw in a prolonged war of attrition. Though successful at certain points, state repression in El Salvador was on the whole counterproductive.

Use of Force Must Be Questioned

One problem with applying a rational actor, opposition/reaction model to state violence in the domestic political setting is that this approach assumes a priori that the state has enemies it must deter with force. Why assume this? How would such a situation develop, and what measures could a state take along the way to prevent it from developing? States, even military or authoritarian ones, have choices between coercive and noncoercive responses to opposition, as illustrated by the Mexican state's alternatingly coercive and ameliorative response to the Zapatista uprising of January 1994. The Salvadoran military-led state of the 1930s through the early 1980s could have appeased the opposition, made concessions, allowed moderate opposition elements to take power, or at least attempted to channel popular mobilization into state-controlled (corporatist) organizations in which the popular sectors would exchange political freedom for socioeconomic benefits. Why was it so consistently coercive instead?

This question becomes especially salient with respect to El Salvador because state violence intensified most rapidly after October 1979, when a reformist coup organized by junior army officers removed the military president from office, brought reformist civilians into the government, and attempted to placate the popular opposition through major redistributive and political reforms. The junior officer corps, led by captains, strongly supported reformist measures, rejected the corruption and brutality of the past, and sought to bring change-oriented civilians into power. Their selection of junta members after the coup and the policies outlined in their "Proclama" were shaped by the Jesuit scholars from the University of Central America. Despite their reformist goals, despite their control of virtually all the barracks in the country at the time of the coup, and despite initially positive steps by the new government to implement reforms and regain popular legitimacy for the state, other state affiliates (the security forces and intelligence units) continued to torture, assassinate, and mutilate thousands of citizens, ensuring that a significant minority of the population viewed the state as so illegitimate that they would wage war against it.

This combination of policies was, to put it mildly, contradictory, and provides clear evidence that we need to avoid thinking of the state as a single, rational entity. Different elements of the Salvadoran state were working at cross purposes, and the elements that favored violence won the day. Moreover, state violence, directed against reformist officials within the state as well as against the population at large, played an important role in driving reformists from office and vetoing their strategy. The targeting of violence against civilian and military reformist leaders, against relatively moderate opponents who were seeking a non-violent solution, and against beneficiaries of the socioeconomic reforms that were carried out in March 1980 all suggest that state violence was not only a response to opposition but also a means of competition for state power, a way of blocking reformist impulses and reformist leaders. All of this suggests that to understand why El Salvador suffered such atrocious violence, we need to look closely at the politics *within* the state to understand why moderation died and how coercion became the state's predominant strategy.

One explanation for this bias toward coercion has to do with the economic and social structure of the country. A number of scholars have noted an elective affinity between economies based on export agriculture and internal repression. Repression is particularly likely to occur where modern export agriculture was

Constitutional Law Did Not Always Prevail

With all of the killing that went on in El Salvador, one might wonder what the national legal system was like. Did the country have a constitution? Indeed it did. Since gaining its independence in 1824, El Salvador has had twenty-three constitutions. Its earliest ones were pioneering examples of progressive thought, and later ones favored progressive thought as well. However, as Karen Racine notes in the *Encyclopedia of Latin American History and Culture*, El Salvador's constitutions have been "documents designed and decreed from above. . . . The documents often bear little resemblance to the society they are intended to govern . . . they have no roots in tradition." Despite their progressive ideals, the constitutions did not prevent the desperate turmoil that overwhelmed the country in the latter part of the twentieth century.

In neighboring Guatemala, constitutions were written less often and with more of an authoritarian flavor. Despite the constitutions, dictatorship was the rule for much of the country's history. An exception was the constitution of 1945, but it was thrown out during the 1954 coup. From that point until the time of the nation's genocide, the conservative elite and the military joined to exercise power however they saw fit.

established through expropriation of communal or municipal lands. Peasants displaced from their lands have little alternative but to work for low wages, helping to make production of export crops highly profitable for large landowners. The result is a highly stratified society in which rural workers are extremely poor and agrarian elites are extremely wealthy. Such elites have vested interests in continuing to repress and exploit rural workers and accumulate sufficient economic and political power to demand that the state continue to deliver the needed levels of repression while eschewing economic reforms.

Social Elites Maintained Repression

This structural explanation for state repression fits the El Salvador experience pretty well. Nonetheless, it is not fully satisfying for two reasons. First, this argument fails to examine *how* conservative economic elites impose their preferences on the state. There were, in fact, many junctures during the 1932 to 1979 period during which strategic elites within the military seemed poised to carry out major reforms in an effort to gain greater popular legitimacy and move away from coercion as a basis for governance. Yet these efforts failed every time, and reversals of reformism were accompanied by greater repression. Clearly the military state achieved little autonomy from social elites. The question is, why? How did social elites succeed in suppressing alternative models of governance favored by strategic elites within the state, especially when they held themselves apart from overt political participation?

Understanding the relationship between social elites and the military becomes all the more central when we consider the peace accords signed in El Salvador in January 1992, in which the civilian government of the National Republican Alliance (ARENA), representing the country's conservative elites, committed itself to radically reduce the legal powers and independence of the military, purge the military of violent and corrupt officers, dismantle the existing military-controlled internal security forces, exclude the army from responsibility for maintaining internal order, create a completely new civilian police force designed to safeguard the rights and safety of citizens, and incorporate the erstwhile guerrillas into the political life of the country as a legal party. These major reforms were accompanied by the creation of a new State Council for Human Rights (Procuraduría de Derechos Humanos) and modifications to the judicial system to make it more professional and less subject to political (and military) control. Taken all together, the agreements, whose implementation was supervised by an observer mission of the United Nations, greatly reduced the state's freedom to use coercion.

The decision to abandon coercion is all the more remarkable when we consider that the ARENA party originated in a conservative political movement that organized death squads and advocated a hardline response to leftist and reformist opposition. Why would a government of this party, funded by members of the conservative social elite who had resisted military reform for decades, sign away many of the coercive powers of the state? To reconcile this event with structuralist explanations of state violence, we must either show that the structure of the Salvadoran economy changed in some fundamental ways during the 1980s or consider the possibility that it was not so much the interests of social elites but rather the nature of their relationship to the state that generated the propensity for state violence.

To account for all of these anomalies, I find it helpful to disassemble the state analytically, examining state factions and their relationships with each other and with different components of civil society. A central theme of this [viewpoint] is the notion that the Salvadoran military state was essentially a protection racket: the military earned the concession to govern the country (and pillage the state) in exchange for its willingness to use violence against class enemies of the country's relatively small but powerful economic elite. To put it another way, state violence was a *currency of relations* between state and non-state elites. . . . Military leaders used conspicuous violence against civilians from the popular sectors in order to manipulate economic elites and preempt them from challenging the authority of the military. For almost five decades this strategy proved successful in maintaining civilian elite acquiescence to military rule. This strategy had costs, however. The mercenary relationship of some state agencies to economic elites and the use of violence for political manipulation cut both ways: private elites retained enough allies within the state to mobilize increased state violence at crucial moments, vetoing socioeconomic concessions by reformist military or civilian state elites. The state as a whole proved unable to break out of the protection racket model of state/society relations at the elite level because the leaders and agencies that were most involved in the violence developed vested interests in continuing a repressive strategy. This was to prove the military's undoing: by failing to achieve broader legitimacy and by using extreme and provocative violence against regime opponents, the military helped create an enemy that it could not defeat. In the end, the military forfeited its privileges, even those it had enjoyed within the nominally civilian-controlled governments of the 1980s, because it failed to defeat the FMLN.

Standing Firm for Religion-Based Causes Was Fatal in El Salvador

Tommie Sue Montgomery

The most infamous assassination during the war in El Salvador was the killing of Archbishop Oscar Romero. In the following viewpoint, a scholar maintains that at the time of his appointment as the top religious leader in his country, Romero was thought to be a rather passive ally of the ruling elite. However, the author explains, in Romero's new position, he quickly became a spokesman for the rights of the oppressed poor people. His radio broadcasts were soon the most-listened-to program in El Salvador. The right wing ordered him murdered, but his message ultimately lived on. Activist, author, and scholar Tommie Sue Montgomery has taught at Brooklyn College and City University of New York.

The selection of Monseñor Oscar Romero, bishop of Santiago de María, as archbishop of San Salvador was greeted with widespread dismay throughout the archdiocese. The old archbishop, priests, religious, and laity had hoped that Arturo Rivera Damas, the auxiliary bishop since 1960, would be chosen. But Rivera had too many enemies going back to the mid-1960s, when the oligarchy had accused him (erroneously) of ghosting

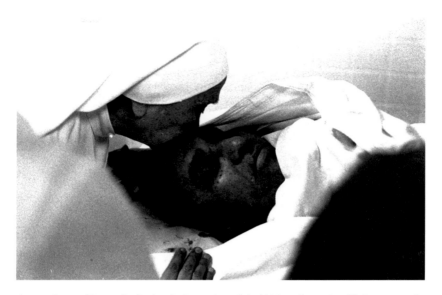

A nun plants a kiss on the forehead of assassinated Archbishop Oscar Arnulfo Romero at the Hospital of Divine Providence in San Salvador, March 25, 1980. The activist anti-violence Roman Catholic cleric was shot to death as he celebrated Mass. © AP Images/Eduardo Vazquez Becker.

Archbishop [Luis] Chávez's pastoral letters. Then he had incensed the government when he confronted Minister of Defense [Fidel] Torres over the abduction of Father [Jose] Alas in 1970. In the meantime he had strongly supported the pastoral line of the archdiocese and had spoken out forcefully against official repression. So when the papal nuncio, being of a mind similar to that of the oligarchy and the government, asked the minister of justice which candidate he preferred, the choice of the powerful was Romero. Romero, who was born in San Miguel, three hours to the east of the capital, had spent most of his priestly life in the eastern section of the country. He was considered to be quiet and noncontroversial. His detractors considered him an ally of the oligarchy and were extremely worried that he would halt or even try to reverse the process of evangelization that had been developed during the previous eight years.

A month before Romero's installation, Rivera Damas was in Rome, where he was informed why he had been passed over. "We don't want anyone who is going to oppose the government," a cardinal with some responsibility in the selection process told him. . . .

Romero stunned everyone by wasting no time declaring where he stood. But it was the [March 12, 1977] assassination of [Jesuit priest Rutilio] Grande only three weeks after his installation that turned Romero into an unflinching prophet of the church. In an interview three months before his death, Romero described his process of "transformation":

I have always tried to be faithful to my vocation, my priesthood. My fidelity to the Church's orientations (and to those encyclicals and council documents that asked for a larger service to the people) has always been the rule of my priesthood. The poor people didn't take me by surprise; I have always felt a preference for the poor, the humble, and believe that in the trajectory of my priestly life it has been like one facet. I wasn't aggressive against the powerful classes when the government was, perhaps, a little diplomatic, and I still have some friends among the very powerful, but a lot have been lost.

There were times when the old archbishop, Mons. Chávez, was suffering the expulsion of priests and couldn't make himself understood with the government; they wouldn't pay attention to him. I felt we should defend this position; the following month after my arrival Fr. Rutilio Grande was killed, which also reinforced my decision because Fr. Rutilio, before his death, was with me by my side in a priests' meeting, the first one I had.

I asked them to help me carry on with the responsibility; there was a lot of enthusiasm from the clergy to help me and I felt that I would not be alone taking care of the situation but that I could count on all of them and that union with the clergy vanquished all our fears. They had the idea that I was conservative, that I would maintain relations with the government, with the rich, and that I would ignore the people's problems, the repression, the poverty; I found here many committed clergy and communities that thought a lot about the situation in the country. Some of them feared I would stop everything and asked what I was thinking of doing. My response was that they should continue and that we should try to understand each other well, and to work in a promotion of the Church's work as Vatican II and Medellín had asked us to do.

Fr. Grande's death and the death of other priests after his impelled me to take an energetic attitude before the government. I remember that because of Fr. Grande's death I made a statement that I would not attend any official acts until this situation [who had killed Grande] was clarified. I was very strongly criticized, especially by diplomats. A rupture was produced, not by me with the government but the government itself because of its attitude.

I support all of the priests in the communities. We have managed to combine well the pastoral mission of the Church, preference for the poor, to be clearly on the side of the repressed, and from there to clamor for the liberation of the people.

The Archbishop Stayed True to the Poor

Romero understood well why this commitment would cause him and other priests to be labeled subversives; the moment the issue of defense of the poor is raised in El Salvador, he remarked shortly before the inauguration of President [Carlos] Romero, "You call the whole thing into question. That is why they have no other recourse than to call us subversives—that is what we are." Archbishop Romero declined to attend the inauguration of President Romero on July 1, 1977, reasoning that it was preferable to risk exacerbating hostilities than to appear and thereby bless a system characterized by fraud, corruption, and repression.

During Oscar Romero's three years and one month as archbishop, the role of the church in the political life of the country expanded with each succeeding crisis. At the same time, under ever-increasing difficulties brought about by waves of persecution against priests, religious, and CEB [Christian Base Communities] members, the church itself was growing and was having a greater and greater impact on the life of the average Salvadorean—which is to say, the poor. While Christian Base Communities multiplied, the focus increasingly was on the diminutive archbishop of San Salvador, both within and outside the country.

Romero's message reached into almost every corner of the country (as well as Guatemala, Honduras, and Nicaragua) via the radio station of the archdiocese, YSAX. Within a short time, the 8:00 mass on Sunday morning became the single most listened-to program in the nation. In second place were YSAX's commentaries, written by as many as twenty different people whose identities were a carefully guarded secret. In third place was Romero's weekly interview. All these programs were broadcast three times in order to reach the largest possible audience.

Romero's Sunday morning mass provided many lessons; but for the social scientist perhaps the most striking was that the mass had become a means of socialization. Although the mass rarely lasted less than two hours, hundreds came and sat on hard wooden pews for the duration—or were glued to their radios. Philip Land, a U.S. priest, related that having been given the extraordinary advice not to attend the mass because the people were too restive and one could never tell what might happen, he wandered into San Salvador's Central Market, where he found that almost every stall had a radio—and every radio was tuned to YSAX. It was a common practice in villages, when no priest was present, to gather in the church and turn on the radio. In some villages the mass was broadcast over the ubiquitous loudspeaker system in the plaza.

Romero Spread the News

All of these people were waiting for "Monseñor's" homily, which generally ran an hour and a half. Each sermon had an invariable pattern: He began with a theological exposition—always with three points—on the scriptural readings of the day. Then he would relate the scripture to the reality of life in El Salvador.

This was followed by church announcements, then a recitation of the events of the week just ended, including a reading of every documented case of persons who had been killed, assaulted, or tortured (by *any* group on the left or the right) or who had disappeared. The Salvadorean reality, however, ensured that the list of attacks at the hands of the government's security forces and the right-wing terrorist groups was many times longer than those by left-wing guerrillas. When an event, such as the coup of October 15 or the promulgation of the agrarian reform, warranted it, Romero would conclude with a "pastoral position" on the question.

These homilies, then, were not only religious instruction for the people, but they were oral newspapers as well. As such they were a potent force in El Salvador from 1977 onward. Just how potent can be measured by the fact that the YSAX transmitter or antenna was bombed ten times in three years—twice in January and February 1980. It should be added that the archdiocesan newspaper, *Orientación*, was also the recipient of several bombs after Romero became archbishop. In spite of or perhaps because of the attacks, circulation almost tripled in the first half of 1977 and had surpassed 12,000 copies per week by early 1980.

The Church Encounters the Wrath of the Government

We have seen that the church in El Salvador, against opposition in its own ranks and from the larger society, became a powerful advocate of political and economic change in Salvadorean society. Its emergence as a political actor during the 1970s was the result of a political and economic reality that contradicted in every respect the traditional social doctrine of the Catholic Church as laid down in encyclicals and conciliar documents and by the Latin American church itself. Its increasingly vocal opposition to and condemnation of official repression and the refusal of the government to implement desperately needed reforms; its unequivocal support of the right of the people to organize themselves to

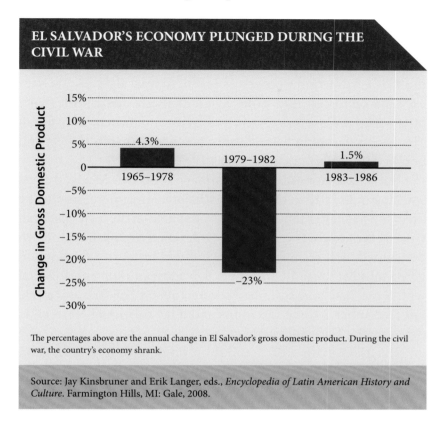

EL SALVADOR'S ECONOMY PLUNGED DURING THE CIVIL WAR

Change in Gross Domestic Product

- 15%
- 10%
- 5% — 4.3%
- 0
- −5%
- −10%
- −15%
- −20%
- −25% — −23%
- −30%

1965–1978

1979–1982

1.5%

1983–1986

The percentages above are the annual change in El Salvador's gross domestic product. During the civil war, the country's economy shrank.

Source: Jay Kinsbruner and Erik Langer, eds., *Encyclopedia of Latin American History and Culture*. Farmington Hills, MI: Gale, 2008.

demand better wages and working and living conditions; and its criticism of the oligarchy for condoning and cooperating in the repression while opposing the right of organization—all brought down on the church the wrath of the government and oligarchy alike. The fact that Archbishop Romero also condemned the terrorist activities of the left was ignored by the right.

The price the church has paid for its effort to be faithful to its understanding of the Bible and of church doctrine is high indeed. Rutilio Grande is usually counted as the first assassinated priest; but Father Nicolás Rodriguez was abducted by the National Guard on January 2, 1972. His dismembered body was found several days later. Arturo Rivera Damas has said that at the time the church accepted the government's explanation that

Rodriguez's death was the work of unknown assailants because "we couldn't believe that they could kill a priest." Between March 1977 and June 1981 ten more priests and a seminarian within a month of ordination were assassinated. At least sixty priests were expelled or forced into exile. Some of these, along with many others who did not leave, were picked up and beaten or tortured. The Jesuits' house in San Salvador was sprayed with bullets and bombed on three occasions.

Nuns have not escaped. In January 1980 two Mexican nuns working in the parish of Arcatao, Chalatenango, were recalled by their superior after they were taken and held in the local National Guard barracks for several hours. Only when Archbishop Romero demanded their release were they brought into San Salvador and given into his custody. In June a Salvadorean nun was attacked with a machete and sustained severe cuts on her face and neck. On December 2 three U.S. nuns and a lay missioner were murdered by the National Guard.

The assassination of Archbishop Romero during a Mass on March 24, 1980, by a professional "hit-man" hired by the extreme right, was only the most heinous of the attacks on the church. His death silenced the most forceful voice for justice in El Salvador. But if those responsible for his murder thought they would silence the church by silencing "the voice of those who have no voice," they were mistaken. They did not understand what Oscar Romero knew very well: "I am not the Church," he would say, "The hierarchy is not the Church; the Church is the people."

US Aid Supports a Protracted Massacre in El Salvador

Thomas Sheehan

In the following viewpoint, a professor asserts the United States sent more than $1 million a day to the government of El Salvador in the 1980s. Yet, the author argues, US politicians expressed surprise and dismay that innocent people, including priests, were killed. The author notes that the killings continued, and US officials merely slapped the wrists of the Salvadoran government. Thomas Sheehan has taught religious studies at Stanford University and philosophy at Loyola University Chicago.

The lesson Americans should learn from the death-squad murder of six Jesuit priests in El Salvador is very simple: You get what you pay for.

Rev. Ignacio Ellacuria, the president of the Jesuit University there and one of the victims, was always very clear on this fact. When I last saw him in El Salvador, he returned time and again to the theme of the U.S.-backed counterinsurgency in that country. "America pays for this war," he said, "and America gets the kind of war it wants."

I knew Ignacio Ellacuria personally. I can say confidently that what would have disgusted him most about the post-mortem on his brutal killing is the sad-faced hand-wringing that Americans ritually engage in after such murders.

I mean the senators and congressmen, decent men and women all, who so sincerely condemn the slaying, but then continue to finance the war. I mean the TV pundits who lower their voices and furrow their brows as they report the murders of the priests, but then avoid telling us why there is a war in El Salvador.

Instead of such hypocrisy I think Ignacio Ellacuria would have appreciated much more the forthrightness of an Elliot Abrams. During the years that Abrams was in charge of the State Department's Latin America desk he made no bones about the fact that the war in El Salvador was a dirty one and you couldn't fight it with clean hands. He even told William F. Buckley that he would not hesitate to fudge a country's human rights record in order to keep U.S. money flowing.

Better to be honest about the blood on your hands than to pretend innocence as you wring those hands and weep crocodile tears.

US Policy Ignores Reality

If Americans are willing to send more than a million dollars a day to the right-wing government of El Salvador to win this war at all costs, then we shouldn't be surprised when the Salvadoran army kills over 60,000 civilians to carry out our wishes.

If Americans are willing to fund such security forces as the Salvadoran Treasury Police, whose members double as the most notorious of that country's death squads, then we shouldn't be surprised when those same police search the Jesuits' living quarters on Monday afternoon and then return on Wednesday night to kill them. You get what you pay for.

The U.S. administration usually defends its innocence in such matters by proclaiming that it wants the Salvadoran army to fight a clean war but by golly sometimes a few of them run

Economics for El Salvador and Guatemala Starts in the Fields

By the 1970s, El Salvador was the most industrialized nation in Central America; however, agriculture remained the mainstay of its economy and coffee the nation's most important crop. Inequality in the country's wealth has been longstanding, with about half the income going to only one-fifth of the population. Many Salvadorans work in other countries and send money to their families back home; about a third of households in the country receive such remittances. Approximately 64 percent of the population is now urban, and in Internet use, El Salvador ranks 107th in the world.

Like its neighbor, Guatemala has long depended on agricultural exports to sustain its economy. Along with coffee, its chief crops include bananas, sugar, and cocoa. Overall, Guatemala has the largest economy in Central America.

Yet income inequality is stark. More than half of the population is officially below the poverty line, and, as in El Salvador, half the income goes to the wealthiest 20 percent of the people. About half of Guatemalans live in urban areas, and in Internet users, Guatemala ranks seventy-second.

amok and kill innocent civilians and we do sincerely regret that and will do our best to stop it next time.

Does anyone swallow that line? Does anyone believe the unnamed U.S. official who told *Time* magazine after the murder of the Jesuits, "We've been telling (Salvadoran) army officers that they can't allow this kind of thing to happen (but) they still haven't learned."

No, the point is that they have learned. They know perfectly well that the money will keep flowing from Washington to San Salvador, no matter what the army and its death squads do. After about $4 billion in aid, after 1 percent of the population of that tiny country has been wiped out (that would be equivalent

A US military adviser trains a Salvadoran Air Force cadet in April 1983. Critics charge that US support and training of soldiers helped extend the period of violence and massacres. © Bettmann/Corbis.

to killing every human being in Cook County [Illinois]), we Americans still allow our representatives not only to continue military aid to El Salvador but to increase it. And we get what we pay for.

Ignorance Allows More Killing

Instead of the crocodile tears that our congressmen shed over the murder of the Jesuits while they keep the pipeline open, instead of the pompous indignation expressed by liberal academics while they keep their students ignorant of this our second Vietnam, isn't it time for a protracted national debate—on television, in our classrooms, in the Congress—about the conflict in El Salvador?

Although this is the longest and bloodiest counterinsurgency war that our country has carried out since Vietnam, the majority of Americans seem blissfully unaware that we are into this one up to our elbows. Most of the undergraduates I am teaching this semester declare that they either did not know there was a U.S. funded war going on in El Salvador or do not have sufficient information to make a decision one way or the other about it. It seems one of the blessings of the empire is the privilege of being ignorant about the world we control.

It was against such ignorance that Ignacio Ellacuria fought all his life. He published the two best journals on current political affairs in El Salvador, he lectured frequently in the United States, and he lobbied Congress for a negotiated solution to the war.

If his death is not to be entirely in vain, if it is not to be the subject of hypocrisy, isn't it time for Americans to find out what they have been paying for in El Salvador and whether they want to keep it up?

After the War, Salvadoran Feminists Aimed to Establish Equality

Karen Kampwirth

In the following viewpoint, a political science professor asserts that many Salvadoran women who were active in the left-wing's fight for human rights found that after the war their male comrades now wanted them to be subordinate. The author cites the story of one young woman who became a political organizer and loyal guerrilla but was forced out when she tried to hold the group true to the ideals of full equality. Such exclusions had the unintended effect of creating an independent and strong feminist movement, she maintains. Karen Kampwirth is a political science professor and chair of Latin American studies at Knox College. Kampwirth is also the author of two books on women and revolution in Central America.

"What do we want? We want equality, nothing more, but nothing less." That was how one member of Women for Dignity and Life (Mujeres por la Dignidad y la Vida, or the Dignas) explained her group's mission as she introduced the festivities at the Dignas' sixth anniversary in July 1996. The quest for equality and nothing less should have been an easy, even obvious, demand for a group that, like the vast majority of the groups that made up the women's movement, had been created by one of the guerrilla groups that made up the FMLN [Farabundo Martí National Liberation Front] in the eighties. After all, social equality had been one of the guerrillas' central goals all along. Yet it was not so easy. It was one thing for women to form organizations in the eighties, under the auspices of the guerrillas, to support the general struggle for social equality. It was quite another when those same women tried to extend general values of social equality to their own personal lives. Many of their former comrades-in-arms responded very badly when they resisted the return to the traditional gender inequality that had characterized life before the war. "They called us traitors, [saying] that we had betrayed the blood of the comrades who fell in battle" (interview, June 28, 1996).

Had the members of the Dignas (and the thousands of women in other groups that also sought autonomy from the guerrilla organizations) really betrayed the blood of the martyrs? The answer, if there is one, requires considering why blood was shed in the first place. Certainly the original motivations for the guerrilla struggle had little or nothing to do with gender equality in an explicit sense. Even the women who later became the most committed feminists had been motivated by the same goals that motivated other men and women when they joined the guerrilla struggle, goals such as democracy, equality, social justice, an end to the dictatorship, and new opportunities in life. Yet once the war ended in a negotiated settlement in 1992, the contradiction between those goals and the reality of continued gender inequality even within the guerrilla organizations, led some to believe that being true to the martyrs required, ironically enough, seeking autonomy from the guerrilla groups and the political parties they became. To be revolutionary meant breaking with the revolutionary leaders. . . .

Yamilet's story is a nice illustration . . . of how young women were mobilized into the guerrilla movement for reasons similar to those that motivated their male counterparts but who, over the course of their participation, came to reevaluate their goals, coming to see gender justice as an essential component of social justice. Yamilet was born in San Salvador in 1961 to "a peasant woman who migrated to the city when she was very young to make a living, and a man who was a salesman, who abandoned my mother after she became pregnant with me" (interview, June 26, 1996). While they were poor, Yamilet's mother worked up to four jobs at once to make sure that her daughters could attend high school.

Yamilet was a student at Young Ladies Central (Central de Señoritas), a public institute, in the second half of the seventies, the same time that the urban social movements that had characterized opposition politics in El Salvador throughout the twentieth century were on the upswing. While she was not an activist, at least not initially, she could hardly ignore the changes in the world around her: "I think I was a normal girl who studied, had fun, had friends; we would go out together, but there was this special situation, there was a rise in the activism of the student movements. I did not participate directly, except for a few demonstrations that I attended. And also there were church movements in my neighborhood. I taught catechism to children. I distributed the church magazine *Orientación,* and that magazine was persecuted. I belonged to a youth group in my neighborhood: we would get together, we would sing, we held retreats, and we would reflect." Yet even though her volunteer work was largely confined to church groups, that did not protect Yamilet from the growing government violence around her: "I remember that one time a man went to a meeting of a group we belonged to and he was from a group—ORDEN—that was one of the most evil organizations in El Salvador. He was armed and drunk at the meeting. He came into the youth meeting and he started to say incoherent things to us; he showed us his ORDEN membership card that had been authorized by a military officer; he showed us his gun. That is, he did not directly threaten us but just by being

In the jungles of El Salvador in 1982, a female guerilla fighter instructs fellow rebels on the use of a US-made automatic rifle. © Sebastian Rich/Corbis.

there without any reason and talking incoherently . . . it made us afraid."

Dangers Surrounded Students

Many residents of San Salvador were afraid in the late seventies. Yamilet and her friends all knew something was wrong but nobody spoke of it. Yet the signs were all around them.

> For example, we knew that dead bodies would appear on the street, that our fellow students would disappear, that some demonstrations had been repressed—for example, the student demonstration of 1975. I was very close the day of the demonstration and the only reason that I didn't go was because the school closed its doors and did not let anyone leave, and that was how we were saved, really, because that was one of the biggest student massacres. . . . So I had no direct tie with any student movement but reality has a way of getting out.

And in her very physical surroundings, her neighborhood in a poor suburb of San Salvador, there was yet another sign:

huge shantytowns sprung up on the outskirts of the neighborhood, populated by refugees from the violence in the countryside. Reading all these signs, Yamilet decided that if she wanted to go to college in peace, she would have to leave El Salvador. For despite the hopes of her new neighbors, city dwellers were hardly immune from the government's wrath and students living in the city were at especially high risk.

So when a friend told her of scholarships for study in the Soviet Union, Yamilet rushed to apply. Luckily, applicants did not have to be affiliated with the Communist Party; what mattered was their performance on a series of exams. As she did well on those exams, she was awarded one of the forty or forty-five scholarships offered that year. Shortly afterward, in September 1979, Yamilet left for the Soviet Union with the intention of spending the following four years studying psychology. Instead, Salvadoran politics found her. Shortly after she arrived in the Soviet Union, the civil war between the FMLN guerrillas and the military-dominated government began back home. From a distance she and her fellow students became involved: "We worked within an organization of Latin American students and of course we were supporting the liberation movements. We would work and send money through the Communist Party, which was our contact." In 1982 a delegate from the party asked "if I would be willing to return to El Salvador to join the armed struggle. I told him yes. . . . It was already 1983 when a telegram arrived . . . saying that I had to be in Moscow in a week. . . . [From there] we went to Nicaragua. In Nicaragua we received training for a few months. I was organized within the Communist Party. All five parties [of the FMLN] were in Nicaragua" (interview, June 26, 1996). By the end of 1983 she had finished her training and illegally returned to El Salvador, by way of Guatemala, where she worked at the front, following the government's radio communications, and later as a political organizer for the Communist Party, one of the five parties of the FMLN, eventually becoming one of the first members of a women's group—ADEMUSA [Association of Salvadoran Women]—that was founded by the Communist Party in 1988 to support the war effort.

From the beginning Yamilet participated in ADEMUSA, ceasing to participate only during the months she spent in prison in 1989 and 1990. But unlike some of other women's movement activists, Yamilet was very reluctant to rebel against the party. In the last days of the war and the first days of peace, she was optimistic that she could successfully carry out what is called double militancy, working both within the party and within the women's movement. Yet as long as her group, ADEMUSA, was beholden to the party, it was very hard to fully advocate for women's rights: "They always put off our activities. That was a process at the level of the institution but also at a personal level. I stopped insisting on promoting the women's movement within the party because I felt that it wasn't possible. . . . It was not a priority." Yamilet as an individual and ADEMUSA as an organization tried to keep their feet in the worlds of both the party and the women's organizations longer than some. But when Yamilet became the director of ADEMUSA, in June 1993, it was finally time to cut all organizational ties with the Communist Party: "We decided that we were not going to go around dressed in party colors. . . . [But there were] costs for us. They said that we were looking for a fight. . . . [In one] press conference they said that I was a traitor. That was really something" (interview, June 27, 1996).

In reacting to ADEMUSA's request for independence by calling Yamilet a traitor, the leaders of the Communist Party inadvertently helped consolidate the autonomous feminist movement. Had she been treated differently, Yamilet probably would not have broken her personal ties to the party. But when her announcement that ADEMUSA sought autonomy was equated with treason, she decided to devote herself exclusively to the women's movement. While it was initially hard to break with the past, the benefits of autonomy were soon apparent. Yamilet was one of many newly independent women who participated in the Women 94 coalition, a project that would have been impossible only a few years earlier, when most groups were still controlled from above by the parties.

Anatomy of the Counterinsurgency I: From Tactical to Strategic Pacification

Jennifer Schirmer

As the fighting in Guatemala headed toward its peak in 1982, the army introduced a program known as Beans and Bullets. In the following viewpoint, a human rights scholar maintains that people who declared loyalty to the military government were eligible for food aid, but those who did not were eligible to be shot. The author notes this was an improvement from the army's previous brutality and recognition that the military had to do more than massacre people and occupy their land. Human rights scholar Jennifer Schirmer, a lecturer in social studies at Harvard University, is an expert on the conflict in Guatemala.

After the 23 March 1982 coup, the Guatemalan army combined civil-military activity, focusing 30 percent of the effort toward killing and 70 percent of the effort toward providing food and shelter to the survivors—first referred to as Beans and Bullets and later as "Shelter, Work and Food." Additionally, it implemented a five-part strategy that included: (1) an increase in the number of soldiers by a call-up of reserve forces and by

Jennifer Schirmer, "Anatomy of the Counterinsurgency I: From Tactical to Strategic Pacification," *The Guatemalan Military Project: A Violence Called Democracy*. Philadelphia: University of Pennsylvania Press, 1998, pp. 35, 61–63. Copyright © 1998 by the University of Pennsylvania Press. All rights reserved. Reproduced by permission.

Members of a Civil Defense Patrol are inspected by the Guatemalan military in 1983. The paramilitary groups, which were charged with protecting the countryside and home communities, were one of the ways the army exerted control over the population. © Pascal Manoukian/Sygma/Corbis.

forced recruitment of captured indigenous men for soldiering as well as for paramilitary civil patrolling, (2) a campaign of pacification that initially concentrated troops for intensified "killing zone" (*matazonas*) operations (and later expanded to other areas), (3) the establishment of Civil Affairs companies to organize Civil Patrols and to concentrate refugees into model villages, (4) the expansion of the legal justification of counterinsurgency through expanded decree-laws, secret tribunals, and censorship of the media, and (5) a campaign of psychological warfare to win popular support for the army. The Beans symbolized the military government's aid to loyal Guatemalans; the Bullets symbolized the struggle against the insurgency. . . .

If one were to sketch out this dialectic of violence without diminishing the suffering of the victims, without mystifying the actions of the guerrilla,[18] and without obscuring the Army's major responsibility for the massacre campaign, it would look something like this: the Army's lessons in counterinsurgency in

1966–67 established a Cold War threat mentality to organized unarmed dissent and armed opposition forces; guerrilla forces regrouped in the 1970s and re-thought their strategy for a prolonged, more indigenous-based struggle, and by 1975 they began sabotaging Army convoys on the Pan American Highway, assassinating mayors and a key landowner known for his brutality; in 1979 the Army under Lucas Garcia amassed troops in the Ixil Triangle, where conservative elders had requested the Army's support in eliminating the "communists"; in October 1981, the Army amassed troops under Task Force Iximché in Chimaltenango for a strictly military scorched-earth offensive that cost 35,000 lives; the Army's spiraling and often indiscriminate violence instilled resentment and fear among Indian *campesinos,* driving many into the guerrilla camp; by February 1982 the guerrilla forces could count on over 360,000 (and possibly up to 500,000) supporters; in April 1982 the Army began to more systematically attack, escalating and intensifying its Pacification campaigns of scorched-earth killing zones of those communities perceived to be guerrilla-mobilized in order to isolate and neutralize the guerrillas, while drawing refugees down from the mountains with amnesty and food for intelligence networking purposes; between April and October 1982, massacres of thousands upon thousands of noncombatants (estimated to be 90 percent of those killed) by Task Forces were carefully planned, directed, implemented, and tabulated. The subsistence and surveillance base for the guerrilla was destroyed, obligating both the guerrilla and the population to flee to the mountains (or to Mexico), with an army estimate of 20,000 succumbing to the army's offer of amnesty and even more to the Food for Work program.

The primary shift in thinking between the Lucas García years and the Ríos Montt regime was between the counterinsurgent ideologue officers, or tacticians, on the one hand, who believed in all-out 100 percent random slaughter—"blindness and massacre," according to Gramajo—which had expeditiously fueled the insurgency, and the counterinsurgent strategists of irregular guerrilla warfare, on the other, who implemented the combination of more systematic yet still brutal 30 percent of killing zones (in which everyone and every living thing trapped is killed) with 70 percent "soft" elements of pacification in counterinsurgency strategy, utilizing Civil Affairs with its psychological operations. This shift in strategy signified the army's recognition that it was losing the war as an occupying army, and that it needed to act as a national army that killed but killed more intelligently "to get the job done." General Gramajo describes the distinction as one between the "pre-1982 Lucas military *operations* in which there was an absence of strategy—brute force and nothing more" (interview) which only caused resentment among the population, and the post-1982 military *campaigns*, which brought the resultant refugee population under control and defeated the insurgency.

But the military did more. The discovery of the impoverished majority by *desarrollista* officers in the mid-1970s raised a new consciousness about the causes of insurgency. Colonel Oscar Hugo Alvarez Gómez surmised that "subversion comes from social contradictions: there is a higher class and a lower class. . . . And there is much discrimination. We military people committed a mistake: that most of the fruits of the infrastructure, if we can use this word, came only to the capital. We might say it was a huge mistake. A disproportioned development badly planned, or better put, badly executed since it has been well-planned since 1800" (1986 interview). As a result, the 1982 National Plan of Security and Development recognized that the causes of subversion were "heterogeneous, based on social injustice, political rivalry, unequal development, and the dramas of hunger, unemployment and poverty; but it can be controlled if we attempt to solve the most pressing human problems" (Ejército 1982a:1). The ability of the military to transform itself and create a development component of counterinsurgency combat operations reflects their institutional flexibility. But it was a development intimately tied to security; there were no Beans without the Bullets, and "we first needed to impose peace," Gramajo explained. The paternalism and authoritarianism of the military's threat mentality concerning the susceptibility of the Indian to manipulation by "foreign ideologies" would remain fundamentally intact (and would hinder the effectiveness of the Poles of Development).

Penetration of the militarized state directly into the heretofore isolated indigenous village was underway. It was the first time in Guatemalan history when both the guerrillas and the army sought to gain the hearts, minds, and stomachs of the indigenous population. With "the ability of civilian and military institutions to work together"—that is, the combination of military force with "effective political coercion," considered a critical, and winning, element for an "effective administration of counterinsurgency program"—the Guatemalan army "demonstrated an understanding of the political nature of counterinsurgent warfare" (Sheehan 1989: 138). The next chapters show how this new strategy penetrated civilian society on all levels, such that Gramajo could proclaim, "We brought government to the village."

Note

18. Stoll has argued that solidarity explanations for the violence "systematically elide the provocative role of the guerillas." Regardless of the structural factors at work that encouraged political violence in Guatemala, he says, "the chronology of events shows the army repression began in reaction to guerilla actions" with the guerillas minimizing their own responsibility for triggering the escalation of military violence. (1993: 91).

Bibliography

Ejército de Guatemala. 1982a. *Plan nacional de seguridad y desarollo*. PNSD-01-82 Guatemala City CEM 01ABR82 RLHGCC-82.

Sheehan, Michael A. 1989. "Cooperative counterinsurgency strategies: Guatemala and El Salvador." *Conflict* 9 (2): 127–154.

Stoll, David. 1993. *Between Two Armies in the Ixil Towns of Guatemala*. New York: Columbia University Press.

The CIA Contributed to Guatemala's Civil War

Molly Ivins

In the following viewpoint, a columnist argues that the United States was on the wrong side of the conflict in Guatemala and was largely responsible for country's civil war. According to the author, the United States trained many of Guatemala's killers and torturers and, through the CIA, kept up its secret support while lying about its involvement. The CIA even lied to Congress, she maintains, and then punished a scholar who revealed the truth. Molly Ivins was a writer whose column appeared in 350 newspapers.

After 36 years of one of the ugliest civil wars ever recorded, Guatemala has decided to end it all with an amnesty. Allie-allie-in-free. Assassins, torturers, slaughterers and those who did their best to commit genocide against the Mayans, everybody's in the clear. Hey, it's their choice.

For those who believe that peace is much harder without justice, there is one actor in the interminable Guatemalan conflict not covered by the amnesty: the United States government.

It's always interesting to see the U.S. media report something like the amnesty in Guatemala with their hands held

Molly Ivins, "The Sorry Saga of the CIA in Guatemala," *San Francisco Chronicle*, December 20, 1996, p. A31. Reproduced by permission.

behind their backs, whistling innocently. Isn't that nice? The Guatemalans have decided to end their civil war and grant one another amnesty. Nothing to do with us, but so happy for the neighbors.

Of course, we've been in it up to our necks ever since 1954, when the CIA overthrew a democratically elected Guatemalan leader, Jacobo Arbenz Guzman, and replaced him with a series of right-wing governments. This led directly to the uprising in 1960. That the CIA's coup was largely responsible for Guatemala's civil war is beyond question.

Of course, 1954 was not the high-water mark for American sanity on the subject of who might be a Communist. We convinced ourselves that Arbenz was a bad guy because he was not fond of United Fruit, which had regarded Guatemala as a wholly owned subsidiary for years.

So we ix-nay Arbenz and touch off a civil war that killed more than 100,000 people over 36 years, according to the *Washington Post*. But naturally, that was not our only contribution. We trained many a Guatemalan military "leader" at our very own School of the Americas right here in the U.S.A. As the Department of Defense recently admitted, to no one's surprise except that of the American media, the School of the Americas is where we train our Latin brothers in torture, assassination, intimidation and execution. And the CIA goes right on supporting one right-wing regime after another while the totals mount.

The CIA Continues to Lie

In addition to an estimated 100,000 dead, there are 40,000 Guatemalans missing and presumed dead and more than 440 villages destroyed. The *Post* reported that the war has created more than 200,000 orphans and 80,000 widows and displaced more than 1 million people.

We were players right to the end. Colonel Julio Roberto Alpirez is not only a graduate of our School of the Americas; like many other Guatemalans, he also has been a paid agent of the

US President Bill Clinton Admits the Country's Fatal Policy in Guatemala

In a visit to Guatemala City in March 1999, President Bill Clinton was the first US leader to publically acknowledge the country's involvement in the Guatemalan civil war. He stated: "For the United States, it is important I state clearly that support for military forces and intelligence units which engaged in violence and widespread repression was wrong, and the United States must not repeat that mistake." Clinton promised that his government would support democracy, harmony, and reconciliation in Guatemala. These remarks came forty-five years after the United States secretly helped a coup overturn Guatemala's elected government, an event that eventually led to the deaths of two hundred thousand people. Over those forty-five years, forces trained and supported by the US CIA and Army participated in massacres, kidnappings, torture, and other atrocities.

Clinton also visited El Salvador on the same trip, but said nothing there about US financial support for that country's military in the 1980s, when it killed civilians on a large scale during a civil war.

CIA. Alpirez was responsible for, among others, the deaths of an American innkeeper in Guatemala and the rebel husband of American lawyer Jennifer Harbury.

After the CIA lied to Harbury and other human-rights activists about its involvement in these deaths, the agency then lied to Congress. The truth came to the attention of Robert Nuccio, a Latin American scholar at the State Department, who in turn gave it to Representative Robert Torricelli of New Jersey. When Torricelli went public with it, the CIA decided to punish Nuccio, whose career is now apparently destroyed and who was stripped of his security clearance by the CIA. Let me just reprise that: The CIA lied to everybody, including Congress, about its own illicit activities—including complicity in murder—and then managed to punish the person who lawfully and correctly told the truth.

The peace treaty in Guatemala will be signed December 29 [1996], but the CIA grinds on. We read stories constantly saying that morale at the CIA is the pits because the last two directors haven't been part of the "good-ol'-boy network." Aw. Would someone finally take these superannuated James Bond fantasists and get rid of them?

In Guatemala, Counter-Insurgency Turned into Genocide

Marc Drouin

In the following viewpoint, a scholar asserts that genocide might not have been the original goal of the Guatemalan military forces, but by 1982 it had become the result of the army's operations. He scrutinizes what happened in twenty-one villages of indigenous people, and finds that more than 23 percent of the total population was slain. According to the author, witnesses reported in every instance that the army was responsible. He maintains adults and children were victims; many females were raped as well. The evidence also shows a clear pattern of planning before the killings were carried out, he argues. Marc Drouin specializes in research on the conflict in Guatemala.

In the social scientific and legal literature, crisis and war are two recurring factors that are believed to be conducive to genocide. According to rapidly changing or worsening contextual considerations, scholars have concluded that genocidal intent can develop ad hoc and that there need not exist a plan or blueprint indicating how to go about destroying certain categories of people. Though the intention at the outset may not have been the destruction of a protected human group, it may become the goal later on as events unfold in the context of war. In this sense, genocide is very much a dynamic process and scholars have explained, for instance, that ethnocide (the destruction of a people's culture) can escalate into genocide (the physical destruction of a people) when the former is successfully resisted by indigenous populations. Genocide can then de-escalate once indigenous resistance has been overcome.

The March 1982 coup brought Brigadier General José Efraín Ríos Montt to power as the head of a military triumvirate. Upon taking power, the junta suspended the constitution, dissolved the legislative congress, and ruled by decree. A 14-point proclamation defined the military government's priorities, four of which referred specifically to the nation in crisis. In April, a National Security and Development Plan placed all public services under military control, making counterinsurgency the government's number one priority. In June, Ríos Montt named himself president of the republic and commander in chief of the armed forces. By then, the *New York Times* was reporting on the contents of mass graves unearthed in the department of Quiché, including the remains of Indian women and children. According to one Western European diplomat quoted at the time, Indians were "systematically being destroyed as a group".

Building upon its 1981 counterinsurgency operations, the Guatemalan army launched its Victoria 82 (Victory 82) campaign plan on 1 July. Its main objective was to continue with the elimination of armed subversives and their alleged local support throughout the Indian highlands. Of particular interest to military strategists were organisations working with the general population, such as church groups, unions and cooperatives, as well as the growing number of indigenous refugees pouring across the Mexican border with their accounts of indiscriminate killing and destruction. In terms of human displacement, the press reported 2,000 refugees a week making their way into Mexico in

February, the number climbing to about 5,000 by the third week of July.

The military offensive under Ríos Montt called for an increase in the number of troops deployed throughout the highlands and northern lowlands. Organised into 30 light infantry companies, 5,300 additional troops were deployed among pre-existing units and three new mobile strike forces. Of interest are some of the troops' ethnic origins: Victoria 82 called for the transfer to the indigenous highlands of soldiers from Guatemala City and the predominantly non-indigenous eastern departments of Zacapa, Jutiapa, Izabal, as well as Escuintla on the Pacific coast. According to Robert Carmack, 15,000 to 20,000 soldiers were said to occupy the sole highland department of Quiché where over half of the 626 documented massacres attributed to the army by the Guatemalan truth commission were perpetrated. If Jennifer Schirmer's estimates are correct, the monthly death toll in Guatemala rose significantly at the time, from 800 under Lucas García, to over 6,000 under General Rios Montt.

The Intent of the Military

Approximately 11,230 people lived in the 21 Indian communities I studied. Of that estimated total, some 2,713 inhabitants were killed in massacres, for an average death toll of 23.3 percent. In 100 percent of cases witnesses identified government soldiers and paramilitary forces as the perpetrators. In the first three massacres in the sample, discussed previously, young and elderly men were selected from lists, tortured and killed. Starting in February 1982, a month *before* General Ríos Montt came to power, the remaining massacres in the sample indicate a change in the army's *modus operandi*. From that moment onward government forces indiscriminately attacked men, women and children in 14 of the 18 remaining communities. In the same number of cases, entire communities were set ablaze and completely destroyed. Perpetrators tortured and mutilated victims in 15 out

Photos of women and men missing since the genocide of the 1980s are pasted on a wall in front of the National Congress of Guatemala in the summer of 2012. © AP Images/Rodrigo Abd.

of 18 cases, women and young girls being raped systematically between March and August 1982.

Killing rates in the communities under consideration ranged from 3 to 57 percent of their estimated total population, before March 1982, climbing to 83 and 96 per cent by July. At that time a US reporter interviewed three infantrymen in the town of Cunen, department of Quiché. The soldiers were asked how they were instructed to act if women and children were present when they raided a village suspected of harbouring guerrillas. One soldier responded that the order was to shoot them all. "Practically all of them are guerrillas," he said, "so the order is to attack everybody alike." And so Indians were attacked as communities, and Indian women often bore the brunt of the army's violence. According to Jan Perlin, "the systematic, public, massive and graphic perpetration of sexual violence" against Indian women betrayed the army's intent to destroy individual members of their communities, as well as the social ties and group foundations that bound them together.

According to Helen Fein, "intent or purposeful action . . . is not the same in law or everyday language as either motive or function". "*For what purpose*," she writes, "is different from *why*, or *for what motive*" an act is committed. In this way, genocide is purposeful or deliberate as opposed to unintentional. The legal definitional criterion for genocide is therefore intent, not motive, and intent is what distinguishes genocide from a crime against humanity like persecution or extermination. As a subjective element of the crime of genocide, intent is twofold, taking into account the criminal intent required for the underlying offence, and "the intent to destroy in whole or in part" a protected group as such. This second intent is an aggravated criminal intention or *dolus specialis*, and demands that the perpetrator clearly seek to produce the act charged.

In the absence of such direct evidence as formal confessions from perpetrators or the original written orders regarding the destruction of a human group, genocidal intent can be inferred or constructed from perpetrator actions, statements and, in some cases, even circumstantial evidence. From a social-scientific point of view, Helen Fein draws our attention to a perpetrator's "pattern of repeated . . . purposeful action" from which we can infer the intent to eliminate a protected human group. In other words, how perpetrators organise and carry out the killing of their victims can shed considerable light on their intent, that is, the actual purpose of their actions.

The Slayings Were Systematic

Based on the first-person accounts at my disposal, I studied 170 comparative elements in 21 cases of massacre. The objective of the exercise was to determine and analyse recurring patterns, if any, in the way these massacres were carried out. If a comparative element was present in at least 15 of the 21 cases under consideration it was believed to be indicative of deliberation and planning. Although the sample at hand represented only 5 percent of the estimated number of massacres committed by government forces between June 1981 and December 1982, it did indicate patterns of repeated and purposeful action relevant to our understanding of a typical highland massacre in 1982.

By then the communities in the sample were all known to the military because of previous visits by soldiers or other forms of surveillance. On the day the massacres took place, perpetrators arrived on foot early so as to gather a maximum number of villagers in their homes. Access to the communities was controlled or blocked, soldiers carrying out house-to-house searches and gathering community members in one place. Victims were then immobilised using ropes, rendered completely defenceless, to be tortured and mutilated. When the killings began, firearms were always used and victims were both men and women, young and old. Victims' bodies were often left where they fell, to be preyed upon by animals or otherwise desecrated. Following the killings, victims' homes were pillaged, their most intimate belongings stolen or destroyed. Finally, their simple dwellings, built with great effort with materials often carried over kilometres of mountain paths, were set ablaze and the communities utterly destroyed.

Comparative elements in this study also allowed for a better understanding of what happened to survivors who managed to escape these initial massacres. It stands to reason that if perpetrators intended to destroy a protected group, they would continue to attack its members even if their communities and means of sustenance had been destroyed. Such persecution after the fact would also belie the often repeated contention that the army's sole or primary purpose had been to destroy the guerrillas' alleged social base of support. Once highland Indian communities had been razed and a majority of inhabitants killed, there would have been nothing left to support the insurgents and therefore no need to continue killing dispersed survivors. Yet that's exactly what transpired, soldiers killing fleeing Indians from the air and on the ground, for days, weeks and even months after the initial massacres. In terms of repeated, purposeful action, it is also worth mentioning that nine of the 21 communities under consideration were the targets of multiple killings, one community—Río Negro, Rabinal—having been subjected to five separate massacres before finally being razed to the ground.

Living like wild animals, eating roots and bark, many fleeing Indians did not survive. Even if they managed to escape army bullets, men, women and children continued to die from sickness, exhaustion or hunger—in other words, from conditions, according to the United Nations Genocide Convention, calculated to bring about their physical destruction. Furthermore, attacks against survivors not only occurred inside Guatemala, but also took place across an international border. Human rights organisations are said to have documented as many as 60 separate Guatemalan army incursions directed against fleeing refugees in Mexico between 1982 and 1984. The truth commission, for its part, documented five massacres committed in Mexico in 1982 and 1983. Additional massacres like these, carried out in a foreign country against displaced populations, indicate the extremes to which the Guatemalan army was willing to go in order to track and kill people who had already escaped one or even numerous attempts to destroy their communities. These subsequent killings beyond Guatemala's borders clearly allude to the perpetrators' genocidal intentions.

The War Ended, but Guatemalan Refugees Have Few Opportunities

Victor Perera

In the following viewpoint, a journalist details the experience of Guatemalan refugees living in the capital city's main dump in the early '90s. According to the author, some people lived there for decades, making a bare living by collecting and selling scrap materials. Residents in the area said they could make more money in the dump than by working in a factory, the author maintains; the dump was a burial ground as well. Born in Guatemala and educated in the United States, Victor Perera was a journalist, author, and professor.

Marta Verónica, known as "La Flaca" for her tensile thinness, has survived in Guatemala City's municipal dump since she was three years old. She lives with her husband, a shoe salesman who makes $8 a week, and their eight-year-old son in a lean-to, a *champa* put together with old pinewood sidings, worn plastic sheets, bent cardboard, and burlap. In a slightly larger tin-roofed hovel next door lives Marta Verónica's mother, Isabela, known familiarly as Chavela, who moved to Guatemala City from the ladino region of Jalapa. Marta Verónica's father, a highland native who had given up his Mayan identity, lived with her mother for three years, until he died of pneumonia. Since then, Chavela has lived in the dump with a succession of male companions, all of whom she has outlived.

The small shantytown of around fifty hovels sits on the edge of a vast expanse of refuse that has grown fivefold in the past fifteen years, as the capital's population has grown to nearly two and a half million. Of the 1,200 tons of garbage dumped here every day, 900 comes from residential neighborhoods. A major factor in Guatemala City's growth is the ongoing war in Guatemala's highlands between the army's counterinsurgency units and four guerrilla organizations; the war has killed approximately 65,000 Guatemalans of Mayan descent since 1978 and has forced over 1 million more to flee their homes. Paradoxically, another factor behind the mass peasant movements is a surge in population. Demographers calculate that it took over four centuries—until 1950—for Guatemala's indigenous communities to recover their pre-Conquest population of around 2 million. Since the 1950s, the Mayas have doubled their numbers to nearly 5 million, placing added stress on their lands. At the present rate of population growth, their numbers could double again by the first decade of the next century.

Since 1980, as many as 500,000 highland Mayas displaced by the violence and by acute land shortages have made their way to Guatemala City. This exodus followed on the heels of an estimated quarter-million Mayas who fled to the capital in the wake of the 1976 earthquake. Between 1975 and 1987, the city's population more than tripled, from 675,000 to over 2.3 million, making it the most populous capital between Mexico City and Bogotá.

The majority of the displaced who arrive in the city every day seek anonymity in one of the sprawling shantytowns that have sprung up along the edges of ravines where they are vulnerable to mudslides and earthquakes. Thousands of these refugees scratch out a meager existence as part- or full-time scavengers in

Desperately poor men, women, and children search for scrap metal in contaminated water at the bottom of a massive trash dump in Guatemala City in 2011. © AP Images/Rodrigo Abd.

the municipal dump, or *basurero,* officially known by the euphemism "sanitary landfill."

Scavenging in the Dump

On a good day, La Flaca can make five to seven quetzales—less than $1.50—collecting scrap cardboard, glass bottles, and plastic bags, which she sells to recyclers at the going rate of five *centavos* (or less than one U.S. cent) a pound.

As I gaze over the mobs of scavengers picking through the mountains of rotting detritus for edible discards or some valuable find like a necklace, a magnet, a broken watch, I ask La Flaca how her way of life has changed in the thirty years she has been here.

"The *basurero* used to be smaller," she says, "and we all knew one another and respected one another's turf. In some ways it was harder than now: there were fewer materials that could be sold, and people were less careless with their valuables; a silver-plated necklace or a bracelet was a real find then. But there was not as much theft or *envidia* [malicious envy] as there is now, and we all worked hard and helped one another stay alive. Now, look at it."

Again I pass my eyes over the fantastic landscape, taking in the hordes of circling black buzzards and the clouds of flies, the thick smoke rising from smoldering trash fires that release a sour smell of organic putrefaction and chemical waste. On rainy days, when the wind blows from the northeast, the stench is a soiled finger stuck in the back of your throat.

At the center of a huge trash pile, as in a dream, I make out two local ragpickers hassling a Mayan woman in brightly woven native dress for a bolt of colored cloth. The smoke and the pervasive stench seem to leach the sky of all color, much as the pre-monsoon heat and dust storms blot out the sky over northern India. At nightfall, the *basurero* recalls the candescent *ghats* along the Ganges, where hundreds of Hindu faithful are cremated every day. What is lacking here is a saving sense of ceremony, a Vedic epiphany or received gospel to sweeten the bitter pill of social inequity. Most of the scavengers are only nominally Christian, and they do not believe in reincarnation.

The Encroaching Landfill

At the northern edge of the visible dump a four-hundred-foot drop marks the *barranco*, or winding ravine, down which the unused garbage is pushed by the bulldozers. Within La Flaca's lifetime, the basurero has moved north by approximately one kilometer, as landfill and concrete mixed with mountains of waste creep up the canyon walls.

In the middle distance, I make out the larger tombstones of the *Cementerio General,* which spread right to the edge of the ravine. There, in the Jewish section, half a dozen of my relatives are buried. Most of the deceased are kept in full-length coffins for about six years. The remains are then placed in smaller boxes and moved to wall niches, where the rent is more affordable. If the survivors default on the rental, the bones may be removed from the boxes and thrown into a central ossuary; or the coffins may be placed on the edge of the barranco for six months. If no payment is made, they are pushed over the side and tumble down to the bottom of the ravine where the coffins rot or break open. In another two or three years, as the dump creeps inexorably northward, the spilled human vestiges and the decomposing refuse will mingle in a pestilential confluence.

Lives Equalize Amid the Garbage

A dozen yellow vehicles, from an electronic dump truck donated by Germany to mule-drawn garbage scows, empty their contents into a sea of raw slop; bulldozers shove the fresh garbage into enormous mounds of compost, which with no soil to fertilize makes nothing grow. On closer inspection, I see three cornstalks with healthy tassels poking through the refuse at the rim of the precipice. And just as improbably a leafy banana tree grows behind one of the shanties. Archaeologists digging here centuries from now may believe they've uncovered a huge aboriginal kitchen or midden.

Here it's every creature for itself. The ubiquitous black turkey buzzards—zopilotes—have only a few seconds' jump on the human scavengers who swarm in to pick through the fresh deliveries. The scavengers come from everywhere in the highlands, the humid coast, the ladino eastern provinces. A Cakchiquel speaker from Comalapa with a huge moth caterpillar crawling unperturbed on his collar scratches for food in the same trash bin as a sugarcane cutter from the Pacific coast. When I ask him why he left his highland home, the Comalapense assures me the living is much better here. "*La milpa ya no da*," he says—the cornfield doesn't yield anymore. The war's disruption of traditional agriculture together with depletion of the soil from the campesinos' overreliance on chemical fertilizers has contributed to the peasant exodus to the city.

The *basurero* is one of Guatemala's more egalitarian institutions: a newly arrived Mayan refugee and a ladino bachelor of arts down on his luck compete for survival on equal terms. The college graduate comes from Antigua and is a father of four. He explains to me in cultured tones that he can make as much as fifteen quetzales a day collecting glass bottles and cardboard, or twice what he would make slaving away in a factory. Although his income estimate sounds inflated to me, I do not contest it; we exchange business cards and I ask him to look me up in the Hotel Aurora.

Hunger and Desperation Lead to Violence

"The change began fifteen years ago," La Flaca explains, "when the supermarkets and the large refineries began discarding large quantities of plastic containers, and there was money to be made from collecting them. People come from everywhere, and there is no respect for anyone. Last month I found a gold-plated necklace—the most valuable find I'd made in years. I wore it for only an hour before someone almost broke my neck trying to yank it away. The next day I sold it for twenty quetzales, because it was too dangerous to keep."

I ask La Flaca what the greatest risks are in her profession. "Crime," she says without hesitation.

Now there are no rules, and people steal from you or kill you for something worth only a few quetzales. Before, we all knew one another, and our only enemy was a guard who kicked us out unless we gave him a share of our finds. Now people kill one another for nothing. A friend I've known from childhood was carved up in her home and set on fire because she rebuked someone for stealing. And two months ago, men armed with machetes attacked a family of four. The mother was so badly cut up she was crippled and went back to her home in Sololá. There are no more rules. The hunger and desperation are too great, and there are too many of us.

As we speak, her mother is gathering large stacks of cardboard in her backyard. Marta Verónica's latest stepfather works alongside her but cannot keep up with Chavela's nimble hands. In my several visits to the dump, I have yet to find her idle; and she always wears her baseball cap at exactly the same, slightly skewed angle.

Despite La Flaca's concern over the rising violence in the basurero, most people here die of respiratory diseases, severe malnutrition, and drug or alcohol addiction, or they suffocate under tons of debris when they stumble and fall under a bulldozer. The zopilotes rarely lack fresh carrion. In the late seventies, when the death squad killings were at their height, the *basurero* competed with rivers, volcano craters, and clandestine cemeteries as disposal sites for tortured and mutilated corpses. . . .

Ex-Soldiers Prefer the Dump

I am continually surprised by the number of men dressed in old and worn camouflage fatigues. It is impossible to know how many of them have been guerrilla militants or sympathizers and how many are army veterans. In Guatemala's war of counterinsurgency, both sides frequently don each other's uniforms to test the campesinos' allegiance.

I approach a light-bearded young man from the ladino town of Zaragoza, in the Mayan province of Chimaltenango. He wears olive fatigues and tells me he served time in the army after he was picked up drunk by a transport during the town fiesta along with two dozen other revelers. The army replenishes its ranks with routine sweeps of towns and villages during their patron saint's feast day, or *fiesta patronal;* the single men between sixteen and thirty serve three months to a year. Armando and the others awoke in the army barracks of Chimaltenango, uniformed in army olive, with dummy rifles in their hands. After three months of basic training, the army placed Armando on reserve and returned him provisionally to civilian life. As a soldier he made the equivalent of $15 a month. He had been sent on dangerous patrols and saw combat three times. Once, the patrol ahead of his was ambushed by guerrillas and half the men were killed.

Guatemalans Welcome the Return of the Army

In the 1980s, many Guatemalans were terrified of the military because it had become an instrument of genocide.

Yet, by September 2011, many were welcoming the soldiers back into their communities, Damien Cave reports in the *New York Times*. The reason was crime—primarily drug gangs. "It's even scarier now than during the war," one woman told Cave.

Fear of crime was the main reason Guatemalan citizens elected a former general, Otto Pérez Molina, as president in November 2011. Pérez Molina campaigned as a hard-liner against the gangs, portraying himself as "iron fist, head, and heart." As the former national intelligence chief, he promised to apply anti-guerrilla tactics against criminals. He became the first former military man elected president since 1986, when democracy was restored after the genocide era.

Once elected, Pérez Molina had to overcome criticism that he once commanded atrocity-committing troops. He said there was no evidence to substantiate that assertion. "I regard it as an advantage that the 30 years I was in the army gave me the opportunity to know the whole country, to live inside, to be close to the problem," he told a *Christian Science Monitor* reporter. "The training, discipline, [and] order are important attributes when you're in government and need to make decisions."

Armando was lucky and got out alive, but he was emotionally traumatized. Two army helicopters buzzed the *basurero* as we spoke, and Armando tensed up until they went by. "They're on the lookout," he said, eyes bulging with fear. "They don't like us to wear our fatigues when we're out of the service."

Armando assured me he made more money collecting cardboard and plastic than he did from his army paycheck; moreover, he is his own man. He said he had met two of his former officers working in the *basurero,* a retired lieutenant colonel reduced to scavenging to pay his debts and an alcoholic former sergeant. Armando's mother and two brothers are living a few blocks from the dump, also scraping out a living from scavenging. Only his better-off uncles remained behind in Zaragoza, and they occasionally send his mother a few quetzales.

Guatemalans Cope with the Past and Redefine the Future

Beatriz Manz

In the following viewpoint, a scholar relates how one Mayan village is moving forward after the genocide in Guatemala. The author explains how theater—written and produced by youth and their teachers—has helped the community understand and cope with the legacy of genocide. Even as the people of the village work to reconcile the past, the author maintains, they face a tough future as violence continues to resurge. She says the youth of the village find hope through education, but opportunities continue to be limited. Beatriz Manz was a scholar in the small Mayan community of Santa Maria Tzejá and an activist against human rights crimes. Born in Chile, she is a professor of ethnic studies at the University of California at Berkeley.

In Santa María Tzejá [an indigenous Mayan village that was targeted in 1982 during the army's "Scorched Earth" campaign], villagers have taken various paths to address the past, including human rights workshops; providing testimonies to commissions of inquiry, particularly from the United Nations and the

Beatriz Manz, "Treading Between Fear and Hope," *Paradise in Ashes: A Guatemalan Journey of Courage, Terror, and Hope.* Berkeley: University of California Press, 2004, pp. 233–235. Copyright © 2004 by the University of California Press. All rights reserved. Reproduced by permission.

Catholic Church; writing and performing local theater productions; insisting on exhumations; publicly denouncing the crimes in national and international forums; erecting a monument to the memory of those killed; and bringing legal charges against the military in court.

Their devastating experiences—painful to recall and even more difficult to come to terms with—were engaged in an extraordinary play called *There Is Nothing Hidden That Will Not Be Uncovered (No Hay Cosa Oculta Que No Venga a Descubrirse)*, written by young people and teachers, particularly Randall Shea, in the village. It narrates the story of the violence of 1982. After initial angst, disagreements, and fears of reigniting reprisals by the army, the play was performed in the village itself for the first time in the mid-1990s. The performance spurred intense discussions and caused heartbreak, tears, and trauma, but also, most important, accelerated the process of coping with what took place. The play was so powerful that the theater group took it on a national tour, and it is now generally viewed as a proud accomplishment.

Few activities at the secondary school have so energized the students as theater productions. The day of a performance produces great expectation as well as pre-performance jitters, and the entire village gathers. International visitors have come to see *No Hay Cosa Oculta Que No Venga a Descubrirse*, the first and most dramatic of the plays. The BBC has taped the performance and has included it in a documentary under the title *No Es Tan Fácil Olvidar (It's Not So Easy to Forget)*. Another play examines racism and discrimination against the Mayans and the working conditions in the *fincas* [estates], portraying submissive Indians being abused on the plantations. Watching the audience is as fascinating as watching the play. They roar and laugh most heartily when the Indians are portrayed as humble, deferential, and subjugated; the actors lower their heads, not daring to look at the *patrón*—they bow, they thank, they trot willingly at every shouted command. The play, written and directed by the students organized as the "Teatro Maya," has provoked serious discussions about social issues throughout the community. This play was called *This Is How Our Mayan Fathers and Mothers Suffered (Asi Sufrieron Nuestros Padres y Madres Mayas).* The most recent play, *A New Fire Lights Our Way (Un Nuevo Fuego Nos Alumbra),* had its debut performance in February 2003. It was directed by a Santa María Tzejá advanced art student, Leonel Bolaños. With the music of Ravel in the background, the play is a very hard-hitting exposure of domestic violence and other gender issues. As with the first play, which provoked political anxiety, this play will no doubt be controversial and will have some older male critics.

Now There Is Hope

The young people in the village show the greatest promise for the future, especially those who had been in Mexican refugee camps. Many were born and educated in Mexico, became used to a more open setting, and returned with a confidence seldom seen in rural Guatemala. In contrast, their counterparts came of age in a tightly controlled village where military authority and fear prevailed, education was not emphasized, and teenage males were forced to join armed civil defense patrols.

The success of the village since the return has drawn on a few key institutions: the school, the cooperative, and village-wide committees. Santa María Tzejá has established an elementary and secondary school staffed by dedicated teachers from the village who are accountable to an elected parents' committee. These teachers have made a difference. More than one hundred students are pursuing professional degrees elsewhere in Guatemala and even abroad, and many more have engaged a solid basic education. This achievement has created a spirit of hope: Sons and daughters of peasants can aspire to what was unthinkable for their parents.

This impressive educational achievement has a downside as well. A sharpened inequality exists between those who attain professional degrees and those who till the soil, or are unemployed

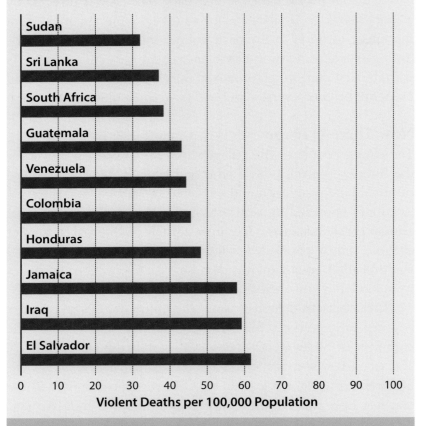

A LETHAL LEGACY FOLLOWS CONFLICTS

Crime grew to replace war in El Salvador and Guatemala, making them among the world's most dangerous countries, at least statistically. Below is a ranking of average annual violent death rates per 100,000 persons in the world's most violent countries between 2004 and 2009.

Violent Deaths per 100,000 Population

Source: Geneva Declaration on Armed Violence and Development, "Executive Summary," *Global Burden of Armed Violence 2011.*

and marginalized. The optimism and self-confidence of educated villagers stands out even to a first-time visitor to Santa María Tzejá; the resentment and despair of those faced with far fewer alternatives has already created problems in this and nearby villages, inflamed by the general lawlessness in the country. A third alternative to enterprising and energetic individuals from both groups is to migrate north. For uneducated youth, migration to the United States provides an alternative to the lack of jobs and land in their own country. For those with professional degrees, migration could become an alternative to not finding a job in their own chosen career. The possibility of working as a construction worker in the United States may look better than being unemployed or underemployed with an accounting degree in Guatemala.

The cooperative [set up and run by the villagers] is less central to the life of the village than it was in the early years, but it still binds people together and creates economic opportunities. Although membership is not mandatory today—nearly half of the villagers have not joined—most of the development projects are channeled through it. Interestingly, Miguel Reyes, the key leader in the refugee camps in Mexico and president of the cooperative in Santa María Tzejá when he returned to the village, is no longer a member. Salvador Castro, another refugee leader and an important leader in the village, also resigned from the cooperative. Nicolás, on the other hand, is an active member and the veterinarian—a critical position. He is also the president of the cattle-raising committee. He is performing these tasks admirably. In 2003, María Hernández, a thirty-three-year-old K'iche', became the first woman president of the cooperative. One of the recent projects of the cooperative is the attempt to commercialize hearts of palm *(palmito pejibaye)*. The women's organization is packaging fruit juice for sale.

An increasingly serious problem throughout Guatemala is a more general lawlessness, fueled by decades of violence and disregard for human life and the law, as well as continued economic hardship and exclusion. Rural gangs have emerged in what previously were villages largely free of violent crime. The result has been imprisonment for some and even the killing of a Santa María Tzejá youth. Getting drunk, taking drugs, stealing, burglaries, raping, and taunting fellow villagers have become more frequent. While Santa María Tzejá may have fewer social problems than other nearby villages, it nevertheless confronts tough, at times shattering, issues; alcoholism has been and continues to be one of the most serious social problems in the village, which exacerbates other social dysfunctional behaviors, such as domestic violence, incest, rape, drug abuse, depression, murder, and suicide.

CHAPTER 3

Personal Narratives

Chapter Exercises

1. Writing Prompt:

Choose one person who is a central figure in this chapter. Imagine you are that person at a crucial moment in his or her life. Write a one-page diary entry expressing your thoughts that day.

2. Group Activity

Divide into groups and come up with three questions to ask perpetrators of the violence written about in this chapter. Then, as a group, discuss how ordinary citizens could deal with potential perpetrators to prevent genocidal repression.

The Early Experiences of a Salvadoran Activist

Leigh Fenly

In the following viewpoint, a journalist details the experiences of Marta Benavides, who became a human rights advocate in El Salvador in the early 1970s. Benavides remembers her early life and how she found the courage to stand up to lethal institutions. She became a teacher while still a teenager and learned firsthand how to lead with few resources amid an environment of fear. Journalist Leigh Fenly is a co-founder of Women's Empowerment International, which has a special interest in Latin America.

When Marta [Benavides] turned 11 and graduated from the neighborhood school [in 1954], a big decision had to be made. Where would she continue her education? For some time the school's director had been encouraging Marta to attend a Baptist boarding school two hours away in Santa Ana, El Salvador's second largest city. Marta began to favor that idea.

It took some convincing, but in time Eva and Teodoro [her parents] agreed, too. One reason was safety. If Marta stayed at home, she would have to take buses alone to the girls' school in downtown San Salvador. It was too risky a proposition. In that time (and through to this day), decisions in the country were always made with consideration for safety.

The school building in Santa Ana was two stories and built around a beautiful courtyard. Surrounding it were gardens and fields with mango trees. The boarding students lived on the second floor in 14 big rooms in one wing; the rest of the building was used for the school. The boarding students, all girls, came from all over the country and from all economic situations. Some were extremely impoverished. The school, the Colegio Bautista, was also attended by non-boarding co-ed students from the local area.

The boarding students were kept to a strict regimen. They went to bed at 9 and got up at 5 to face a cold shower. Each student had a bed, a place at the dinner table, a small closet. Marta was homesick her first year and pleaded to come home, but Eva decided she should stay, and by the end of the first year Marta had gained her footing—and a scholarship.

She earned the title "the girl of the medals," winning awards for best achievement in math, science and for best grade point average. Part of her success derived from her joy in reading. Her tradition when she received her textbooks was not to wait for the chapter-to-chapter assignments, but to devour the whole, cover to cover. She never considered herself more intelligent than the other students; she simply loved to learn new things and apply herself.

A Religious Revelation

On Sundays, she put on the white "church" uniform with its big collar, stripes and a tie around the neck, and walked through the fields and streets with the other students to the Baptist church, with its wide latch windows. The students sat in wooden benches reserved for them. The lessons she heard concerned hell and sinners. She felt the increasing pressure by the church to bring her parents into the fold, so they too could be assured a place in heaven. Her stomach tossed with the idea that her beautiful parents and sisters would be condemned to suffer for eternity in hell.

Troubled and restless, she woke at 4 o'clock one morning, went outside in the darkness and called to God: "OK, I don't know what's going to happen, but my parents are not going to come into this church. I love them too much to separate myself from them. So I'm choosing to go to hell with them."

As soon as the words were out of her mind, Marta felt a calm flow through her. She marveled that no one came after her and no terrible things happened, even though she dared to challenge God. Marta learned then the limitation of religious teachings and that God was bigger than she was being told.

Marta was elected president of the church's Youth Society, which met on Sunday afternoons to do what she considered superficial activities. As president she was ready to bring a little more seriousness to the meetings, to plan things that would help the students prepare for the future. She had been watching at the library as the girls went in giggling to leave messages hidden in books for their boyfriends. She lived with some of these girls and knew many had very little understanding of what it meant to be in a relationship.

Years earlier, Teodoro and Eva had taken the occasion of a teenage pregnancy in the neighborhood to explain to their daughters everything they needed to know about sexuality, the female body and pregnancy. The unwed teen in the neighborhood had been beaten up and kicked out by her family.

Marta's parents assured their daughters that that would not happen to them. On the other hand, should one of the Benavides girls get pregnant, life would not be easy. Eva told them, "You will have your baby and you will have to study at night and work during the day to take care of that baby."

A Lesson in Sexism
Believing that her fellow students needed truthful information, Marta invited two members of the church, a male doctor (a

deacon of the church) and a female doctor, to the next meeting to talk about sexuality and pregnancy. The meeting was very successful and a great deal of information was exchanged.

But Marta soon was called in by the Baptist deacons to tell her that her services as president were no longer required. By broaching such a forbidden topic and bringing it openly to the students, Marta had incurred their wrath. She didn't mind. She knew her parents would have approved and that she approved. No one should be kept in the dark. Marta decided not to leave, but to spend the rest of her time in the group helping the new president plan meaningful programs for discernment and action. No pressure was put on the male doctor, but terrible things were said of the moral standing of the young female doctor, also a member of the church. For Marta this experience was a very clear expression of the moral and sexist practices of the church, which she experienced over and over again throughout her life, not only in her country but in the United States as well. It was also very clearly a matter of justice, and thus an issue of peace.

At Christmastime when she was 16, Marta was on a bus heading to Mexico City. She and five university students, all men, had been chosen to participate in a congress held by the international Union of Latin American Evangelicals Youth (ULAJE). The bus had started in Panama, picking up participating students throughout Central America. It took three days on the bus to reach Mexico City.

In El Salvador, Marta remembers, Protestants (commonly called evangelicals) were definitely in the minority to the reigning Catholic Church. Only the Baptist church had any significant membership; Marta didn't even know that other faiths— Lutherans, Anglicans, Presbyterians and Methodists—even existed. But at the congress all these faiths and more were represented by young college students from South America, the Caribbean, Canada, the United States and Europe.

Her eyes and ears were opened. There was a frenzy of excited discussion of human rights issues. The Mexicans heatedly discussed land rights for peasants and the constitutionally protected *ejidos*–the communally held lands, a heritage from the indigenous practices, which the government was taking away in violation of the law. The Jamaicans and Canadians debated their colonial relationship with England; at the time, Canada's legal name was the Dominion of Canada. The problems of colonialism dominated the discussion by the Puerto Ricans. Caribbean students discussed racism, while Bolivians, Ecuadorians and Peruvians brought the issues of indigenous peoples' histories and rights and how their situation as second-class citizens affected each nation as a whole. Marta listened avidly and made friends with students from other countries and faiths.

As Marta participated in the congress, her fellow Salvadorans watched with worry and fear. One day they took her aside and demanded she stop mingling with these dancing, smoking, drinking *rojos*—reds. At home, everyone who fought for their rights was labeled red, or Communist, and bad things happened to all so-called Communists. Massacres of entire villages had been done in the name of wiping out Communists. The young men told Marta she would be personally responsible if anything terrible happened to them when they returned home. Marta chose to meet with her new friends in less public places, outside the Salvadorans' attention.

A Mind-Opening Experience

When the group returned home, Marta and the young men prepared individual reports to share at church services. Marta stood with them in front of the worship service in silent amazement as these young men together reported her activities. They told the congregation she had consorted with Lutherans, Methodists and other suspect groups. Her actions, they claimed, had put them all in danger. The young men sat down and Marta was not allowed to speak at all. The minister, missionary and deacons did not intercede because they also classified people as reds.

Marta, however, was not silenced forever. Other more open-minded church members sought her out and were interested in what she had seen and learned. She told them she did not regret her actions. She told them how important and meaningful it was for her to have visited Mexico, to meet so many people of so many points of view from different ethnic, social, economic, political, cultural and religious backgrounds, and to see young women voicing and defending their positions, creating meaning and knowledge, and feeling and acting powerful in then own right. "One must not be afraid to have one's feet on earth," she said. And she didn't even mind that she was never invited to ULAJE again.

Becoming a Teacher

Marta raised her hand.

Who in the classroom was interested in teaching literacy? At 17, Marta was.

Representatives from the Ministry of Education had come to Marta's school, offering the students an opportunity to be trained in teaching literacy. After the training, the students would be able to go into the rural areas and impoverished communities to teach peasants to read and write.

At the time the illiteracy rate in El Salvador was at least 60 percent. For decades the military dictatorship had prioritized keeping order over literacy. But literacy training was gaining new prominence because of a U.N. program encouraging all nations to teach their citizens to read and write. The Salvadoran government agreed to participate and sent Ministry of Education representatives to the high schools to recruit volunteers. Marta and a few of her friends embraced the idea.

Marta received two weeks of training but no teaching materials. She heard a refrain that would become common to her ears throughout her life: "Our country is poor. We don't have the money for materials. But you are creative people, you will figure it out." Once the training was completed, the students were on their own. There was no effort to organize them or send them to areas where their new skills could be put to good use.

Marta began at her school. In the beginning, the school director resisted her idea of an evening training because somebody would have to pay for the electricity required to keep the lights on at night. Marta said she would figure that out, and she conducted her first two-week training there as the school year was ending.

Once the term finished, she dispatched herself to a nearby village to begin teaching impoverished coffee workers and their families the lessons she had learned. She traveled by bus, passing rows of crowded huts strung along highways and rivers—on whatever land was left after the large landowners had taken the best for themselves during the conquest and colonial times. At the time, the wealthiest 2 percent of the population owned 60 percent of the land, and most peasants had no land at all.

When she arrived, Marta saw the peasants' one-room huts with thatch for walls and roofs and dirt floors—no windows, no doors. There was no water, electricity or sanitation facilities. The people used kerosene for light and wood for cooking, and they found a place for her to sleep on a small folding bed in the tiny Catholic church. "One kick," she remembers, "and anyone could have knocked down that door." That first night as bats flew over her, in order to sleep she placed her life in the hands of God.

When Marta came to teach the first lesson, the women were sitting on tree stumps nursing their babies. Bats darted in the smoky kerosene light. There were no blackboards. No tables. No chairs. It was futile to think that in these conditions anyone could be taught to read. And Marta knew it. Rather than panic, she turned to what she knew best: her mother's lessons. As Eva had taught her, Marta respected the impoverished people in front of her and viewed them as the backbone of society. "My parents taught me impoverished people were not poor. They had been made to live in poverty. They were picking the coffee the rich people were selling in Europe and the United States."

Going Beyond the Lesson Plan

As she observed the peasants, she found more to admire. No matter how tired and hungry they were, they showed up every night eager to learn. But she also saw there was precious little relief from work in the village. The men drank or went to cock fights; the women stayed home or chatted with neighbors. Seeing this, Marta decided to turn her lesson time into a circle for community, laughter and fun.

She explained to her group of eager students that trying to teach them to read and write was too difficult in these circumstances. She said that reading was not just learning the alphabet and being able to sound out words. Real literacy, she told them, was being able to receive information, create opinions and express yourself. That would need to wait for another time, but they must press to get that right. Still she had much to offer them.

She asked the group for stories. It didn't take long before the men and women were telling tales in low voices that rose excitedly at dramatic moments. They told horror stories, the scarier the better. Many dated from before the time of the colonizers and featured supernatural beings, some animal-like, others human. When the group ran out of scary stories, they told riddles and proverbs and discussed what they meant. As trust built, the people discussed their problems and potential solutions, describing their living conditions and what they wanted for their children and the importance of education. It was a time of joining together, a sacred time for all to share in the community that was theirs.

Marta was witness to the bonding. She recalls, "Intuitively I knew that a community was being created and there was a different level of perspective and that the community would never be the same again because of that circle."

The Upper Class Strikes Back

The view was quite different on the wide verandas of the luxurious plantation houses, where the wealthy coffee growers heard about these meetings taking place throughout the country and grew alarmed. To their minds nothing good could come from peasants meeting regularly and discussing their issues and concerns—and worse, with outsiders: urban students. They acted resolutely to stop it. They contacted their friends in high places, fingering the student teachers; the government followed through decisively.

Suddenly from being a government-sanctioned program, literacy training became a subversive action. The government hunted the student teachers and some were killed. "This was life as we knew it," Marta reflects. "When we were going into the countryside we were not only making friendships, we were breaking the taboo of mixing with other 'classes.' They killed some of us as a precaution, a warning."

The government's actions added one more layer of fear, but it didn't numb Marta to her experiences in the village. She loved the connections she made and felt at home with the people. She observed their power, but also learned how much had been taken from them—and for how long. She saw how they were forced into mere survival. It was the end of the 1950s and by then she and many of the caring youth knew how wrong it was to be deprived of so much, and to have it done most often by force, repression and death—under the guise of keeping law and order, and all under a government, a military regime, that was the result of fraud or a coup d'état.

Who Killed Archbishop Romero?

Craig Pyes

*In the following viewpoint first published in 1984, a private inves-
tigator and journalist discusses the March 1980 assassination of El
Salvador's prominent religious leader, Archbishop Oscar Romero.
Although El Salvador's president, Jose Napoleon Duarte, had announced a commission to investigate the killing—which was widely
attributed to the notorious death squad—justice was not forth-
coming. The reason, according to the viewpoint, was that the main
suspect and leader of the death squad was Roberto d'Aubuisson,
El Salvador's most popular and powerful politician after President
Duarte. Even with a preponderance of evidence, the author states,
a resolution of the case appeared doubtful. Craig Pyes is currently
a senior correspondent for the Center for Investigative Reporting,
specializing in corruption, human rights, national security, and international crime.*

This summer El Salvador's President, Jose Napoleon Duarte,
announced that a presidential commission had been
formed to investigate five political killings attributed to the notorious death squads, particularly the assassination of Catholic

Archbishop Oscar Arnulfo Romero, who was gunned down March 24, 1980, as he conducted mass in his small chapel in the capital. Of all the 40,000 killings in El Salvador during five years of fratricidal war, the slaying of this 63-year-old prelate probably touched the Salvadoran people most deeply. Many poor people still display his picture in their homes, revering him as a martyr who spoke out in their favor and against the atrocities committed by El Salvador's little Caesars.

American and Salvadoran officials regard the probe into Romero's assasination as a touchy business. One of the suspects, extreme rightist Roberto d'Aubuisson, is El Salvador's most popular politician after Duarte, and is the Salvadoran President's chief rival for power.

Two years ago, when Duarte was President of the civilian-military junta, he told reporters that he knew of no evidence linking d'Aubuisson to the slaying. This year, as the Duarte-d'Aubuisson rivalry unfolded on the hustings, Duarte began hinting that his opponent may have had a role in it. In May, right after Duarte assumed office, a source close to the Romero investigation told former Salvadoran Ambassador to the United States Ernesto Rivas-Gallont: "Within four months of Duarte's inauguration we either have d'Aubuisson in jail or he's been cleared." Now Duarte has reportedly let it leak that he will testify before the commission if asked, and that he can link d'Aubuisson to the crime.

There was disagreement among Senators about whether d'Aubuisson's supposed connection to the Romero assassination should be included in the unclassified version of the Senate Select Committee on Intelligence's just-completed investigation into Salvadoran death squads, scheduled for release last week. Democrats charged that Republicans who control the committee fear that if d'Aubuisson's true role is made public, it could hurt the re-election chances of Senator Jesse Helms, whose strong support for the Salvadoran rightist has been raised as an issue by his Democratic opponent, North Carolina Gov. Jim Hunt. Helms has defended d'Aubuisson, calling him a "deeply religious" man and saying that he would disavow him if there was any "credible evidence" linking him to the death squads. Helms has said he doesn't require evidence that would stand up in court, and charges that when he sought "specifics" from Administration officials in the past "they backed down."

Administration sources told me privately that their reluctance to provide "specifics" to the Senator arose out of fear that U.S. intelligence sources might be endangered if their identities were made known to Helms's violent right-wing friends in Central America. Other sources said that the Senate Intelligence Committee shared that concern in choosing which staff aides would work on the report. Helms's recent revelation of classified information that the Central Intelligence Agency was funding the Christian Democrats and his assertion that U.S. Ambassador to El Salvador Thomas Pickering acted as "paymaster" may have provided psychological encouragement to Salvadoran rightists in their abortive plot to kill the Ambassador this spring.

The classified version of the Senator report, which runs hundreds of pages, analyzes U.S. knowledge and procedures regarding Salvadoran death squads, based on cable traffic and internal reports from the C.I.A., the State Department, the Defense Department, the National Security Agency and the Justice Department. A Congressional source who read some of the cables said that what he saw lays out a convinging case that d'Aubuisson is a "main player, the one who directed and controlled" death squad operations. One person familiar with the report said that it shows that the rightist leader is "involved up to his armpits" in the Romero and other killings. "If he lived in this country, he'd be sent to the gas chamber a hundred times over."

The classified report does not attempt to resolve the question of who killed Romero. A different account is provided by each agency reporting on it, and the identity of the triggerman varies. Each account is based on a different source, "each in a position to know," according to people who have read the classified version.

All the accounts agree, however, that d'Aubuisson had a hand in the assassination.

Information linking d'Aubuisson to the Romero killing was first published in April 1983, by this reporter in the *Albuquerque Journal* and by Laurie Becklund in the *Los Angeles Times* as part of a joint investigation. Those accounts were based on the investigation conducted by the U.S. Embassy in San Salvador, whose findings are included in the Senate classified report. A still undisclosed C.I.A. account of the assassination, also considered to be credible, contradicts some of the information in the embassy's report. But the embassy version is important because it comes primarily from a known source whose information proved reliable in the past; because the informant said he participated in the plot; because incidentals of his story were confirmed by an embassy employee; and because all those he named, as well as the source himself, are believed by U.S. intelligence to have been deeply involved in death squad activities.

The circumstances surrounding the embassy's investigation have since been amplified by interviews with U.S. officials and with Congressional sources who have access to confidential State Department cables, and by conversations with Salvadoran military and government officials, including sources close to d'Aubuisson. Because of the sensitivity of the material, all those interviewed requested anonymity.

The U.S. Embassy received its first account of the killing in mid-November 1980, according to former Ambassador to El Salvador Robert E. White in testimony before the House Western Hemisphere Subcommittee earlier this year. He said a "particularly brave and resourceful American diplomat" had met with a Salvadoran Army officer who had participated in the plot and who said he had witnessed d'Aubuisson order the killing. (D'Aubuisson has many times denied his involvement.) The cable reporting this meeting describes the Salvadoran informant as being of unknown reliability. But U.S. officials came to regard him as "highly reliable" because he subsequently identified the

National Guardsmen who killed four American churchwomen in December 1980. Those he named were later convicted by a Salvadoran court—a lonely example of justice being meted out to military men for their participation in death squads.

Embassy personnel came to refer to the informant as Killer, and that's how his telephone calls were announced by cheery-voiced secretaries. "He was a ruthless, evil guy, quixotic, tough and brutal," recalled a U.S. official who was stationed in San Salvador. Although Killer's motivation for talking to the embassy remains unclear, those familiar with his reports said he resented d'Aubuisson and others in the pay of the wealthy families. Killer said the death squads were necessary because government restraints on the security forces compelled soldiers to take extra-legal action. When he mentioned the Archbishop, he referred to him casually and unceremoniously as "that fellow the priest." He said he gave bullets from his own gun to the officer chosen to carry out the assassination, so that he might participate symbolically in the act.

The decision to kill El Salvador's highest-ranking cleric, U.S. officials believe, was part of a planned coup d'etat by the extreme right. The plotters hoped the killing would touch off disorder and panic, which would enable them to seize power and stem the social and economic reforms enacted in early March 1980. "That was a real important time for the right," explained a U.S. diplomat familiar with the Romero killing. "Their backs were up against the wall. They were pushing and kicking. It was like a shark in a frenzy."

Killer said he had been contacted in El Salvador by d'Aubuisson, who in early 1980 moved his paramilitary organization to Guatemala. There d'Aubuisson received financial assistance from supporters of Mario Sandoval Alarcon, chief of Guatemala's ultraright National Liberation Movement (M.L.N.), and from wealthy Salvadoran exiles living in Guatemala and Miami. Those funds were used to sustain a political-military organization in El Salvador capable of carrying on what d'Aubuisson referred to as a "Guatemalan-style" anticommunist campaign, similar to the one in which tens of thousands of Guatemalans had already perished.

A ledger from d'Aubuisson's paramilitary organization, belonging to his bodyguard, Capt. Alvaro Saravia, was seized when d'Aubuisson was arrested for treason by government soldiers at a farmhouse outside San Salvador six weeks after Romero's assassination. Virtually ignored by U.S. intelligence, which did not consider right-wing death squads to be a priority until 1983, Saravia's notebook records in accountant's detail thousands of dollars received and disbursed by d'Aubuisson's organization during the time leading up to and immediately following the assassination. It itemizes payments to hard-line army officers linked to death squads; requisitions of supplies for assault teams, including the types of weapons and the estimated number of bullets to be used; purchases of arms, bulletproof vests, silencers, nightvision scopes, forged identification cards and Guatemalan license plates (for undercover operations); names and flight information for the airborne cavalry of civilian and military pilots who operated an extensive courier and smuggling network between private air clubs in Guatemala and El Salvador; and names and telephone numbers of key operatives, including those of the officer and the triggerman believed to have gunned down the Archbishop.

Another person prominently mentioned in the Saravia notebook was one of d'Aubuisson's most trusted aides, Capt. Eduardo Alfonso Avila, who later claimed he helped plan the Romero assassination. U.S. investigators have identified Avila as a principal figure in the death squad network. He once told an Argentine intelligence officer than his specialty had been executing people by insulin injection. In addition to or as part of his terrorist activities, Avila served with the army's general staff. He was also a contact of a former U.S. defense attache in El Salvador. After he was implicated in the November 1980 failed bombing attempt against liberal army chief Col. Adolfo Arnoldo Majano, Avila was banished to the Salvadoran Embassy in Costa Rica, where he ran intelligence operations.

A cable transmitted to Washington from the defense attache in Panama in May 1982 relates the bizarre story of how Avila came to confess his part in the Romero assassination. While vacationing on Contadora Island off the coast of Panama, Avila suffered what one might interpret as an existential crisis. He had fallen in love with a young Costa Rican prostitute who had learned too much about his past, and he couldn't decide whether to kill or marry her. The cable says he tried to kill her but failed, then in remorse attempted to overdose on Valium but failed, then called for help.

When help arrived, Avila, reminiscent of Lady Macbeth, told the person he was having hallucinations of a bloody figure in black "crawling from the floor" of the San Salvador Sheraton Hotel—a reference to the January 3, 1981, killing of Jose Rodolfo Viera, director of the Salvadoran agrarian reform program, and his two American aides, Michael Hammer and Mark David Pearlman. Queried about what he knew of that incident, Avila reportedly said, "I have killed them as I have killed many others." When pressed for details, the cable says, Avila admitted that "he personally planned and had two others assist him in the killing of Archbishop Romero. He indicated that he had used a dark car on this occasion and that he had spent three months planning the execution."

Avila's statement that the killing had been planned for three months is not contradicted by any other evidence attributed to the embassy. During that time there were several threats and failed attempts against the Archbishop's life. Also, Ernesto Panama, who worked closely with d'Aubuisson in 1980 and served as his press spokesman during the last election, said that as part of their "psychological war effort" they had tried to discredit Romero, who was known to suffer from a nervous disorder. "We tried to find out about when Monsignor Romero was in the cuckoo's nest in Costa Rica," Panama said. "We tried buying the records but we couldn't. They wanted too much money." Civilian members of d'Aubuisson's inner circle, who spoke on background only, also admitted that in the months leading up to the assassination, they blew up the Catholic radio station, which had broadcast the Archbishop's homilies, bombed the Jesuit-run Central American University, delivered death threats to priests and machine-gunned the Jesuits' residence.

One February 24, 1980, a month before his assassination, Romero announced in his Sunday sermon that he had been notified that his name was on a list of those to be killed the following week. His personal diary—quoted in *The Word Remains: A Life of Oscar Romero*, by James Brockman—shows that he was aware that the military was carrying out what he termed "special warfare," killing not only suspected leftists but also their families to stop the spread of "communist" ideas. Each Sunday until he died the Archbishop read the names of those arrested, murdered and "disappeared" by government forces (at that time the toll was upward of 500 a week). He called on the Duarte faction of the Christian Democrats who remained in the ruling junta to resign and stop "concealing for the sake of international public opinion the bloody repression of the people." In a letter to President Jimmy Carter he called for the cessation of American military aid to the Salvadoran government and pleaded for the United States not to involve itself directly or indirectly in Salvadoran affairs. Romero seemed to seal his fate during his last Sunday homily, March 23, when he appealed directly to the enlisted men carrying out the killing to disobey their orders. But by then the preparations for his assassination had passed the point of no return.

Killer told an embassy official that on or about March 22 d'Aubuisson summoned about a dozen active-duty military officers to a safe house in San Salvador and announced that a decision had been made to assassinate Romero. There was so much vying for the honor of carrying out what was regarded as a "sacred duty," an embassy source explained, that it was determined "the only fair way to do it was by lot . . . as though it were some sort of competition for a prize."

All those present at the meeting "were people who worked together officially or unofficially," the source continued. They were part of "that network of really, really bad guys who identified with each other, their ability to be valiant. . . . There's a certain mystique around you if you're macho, and a little cruelty adds to that." Among those reportedly present were National Guard Capt. Victor Hugo Vega Valencia, a d'Aubuisson crony who was later exiled to Mexico as military attache because of his involvement with the extreme right. Saravia's notebook records that Vega received a $1,000 payment the day after the assassination. Another alleged participant in the death lottery was Lt. Francisco Amaya Rosa, a National Guard officer. Lieutenant Amaya and his confederate Lt. Jose Rodolfo Isidro Lopez Sibrian, an intelligence officer with the guard and partner with Amaya in a Central American car-theft ring, have been described by U.S. officials as "action men" for "the most efficient killing machine in the National Guard." Ambassador White told the House Western Hemisphere Subcommittee that Lieutenant Amaya drew the winning lot. Amaya is said to have chosen a favorite triggerman (a "dog," as they are known) to do the shooting.

Late in the afternoon of March 24, in an appearance previously publicized in the newspaper, Romero celebrated a memorial mass for the mother of a journalist friend at his small chapel at the Cancer Hospital. As he was concluding the ceremony, a dark car drove up to the door, and a single shot was fired from it at Romero inside. The bullet struck him close to the heart, and he slumped to the floor. A short time later he died on a table in the emergency room of a nearby hospital.

Until Killer's first report, eight months later, the U.S. Embassy had few details about the assassination plot. It was not until late 1981 that U.S. diplomats learned the name of the alleged triggerman. According to embassy accounts, this happened when Killer was shown a copy of the Saravia notebook by a Foreign Service officer. While leafing through it he stopped at the name "Musa" and is said to have told his handler, "That's the guy who shot the priest."

Embassy sources said that after conducting his own investigation, the foreign Service officer learned that Musa was Walter Antonio Alvarez, a 27-year-old former National Guardsman from Apopa, a small town outside San Salvador. The telephone number listed by his name in the notebook belonged to a downtown department store called Almacenes Pacifico, where Alvarez was employed. Alvarez spent most of his spare time, however, with present and former Guardsmen who served as glondrinas, or foot soldiers of the paramilitary far right.

Alvarez's role as triggerman is one of the weaker pieces in the embassy's investigation, according to U.S. officials, but his history indicated that he was well qualified for the job. Additional information about Alvarez was obtained by this reporter from one of d'Aubuisson's personal pilots, who has proved a reliable source in the past. The pilot had access to d'Aubuisson's inner circle and was in a position to hear things. While evasive about the Romero assassination, he said he believed it was carried out by a low-level military officer "who decided the job had to be done and nobody would have the guts to order it. You know, one of those people who had to be in charge of one of those death squads." He said he remembers somebody mentioning the name of the triggerman, but it wasn't Alvarez. The pilot's version is somewhat consonant with what other sources told me had been reported by the C.I.A. and was contained in the Senate Intelligence Committee's report.

His description of Alvarez is worth repeating, because Alvarez is somewhat typical of the death squad "dogs" used by the higher-ups to kill. The pilot said the former military man earned extra money as the bodyguard of one of the owners of Almacenes Pacifico, who valued him not only because he was an excellent marksman who "had the guts to kill somebody" but because he was happy to do it. (There is no information linking the owners of Almacenes Pacifico to the Romero assassination.)

The pilot said he frequently met Alvarez at the private air club in San Salvador, which was a gathering place for leaders of the paramilitary right. While their bosses were discussing politics and plans, the pilot said, he Alvares and other bodyguards would sit around boasting about their prowess and misdeeds in order "to gain status."

"This guy [Alvarez] was a real hothead," the pilot recalled. "He was just mad as hell" because the Guardia was being restrained and the military wasn't acting tough enough. Once, when Alvarez and his employer were watching a leftist demonstration from a terrace of the department store, Alvarez persuaded the owner to let him take a potshot at one of the protesters. The pilot recounted, without indicating the source of his knowledge, how Alvarez pulled out his gun—a small pistol with a four-inch barrel—and fired at a demonstrator in the street. "Picked him off right from the terrace, with a .38 Special! That's some shot. And he got this guy, and boom! And he was jumping up and down." Then he added:

> He's probably the one person I ever met in this whole movement who probably was really off his head . . . the type of human being that likes to kill, period. He was very shifty-eyed, very unstable. You knew there's something inside the guy that's dangerous and could explode any minute—his eagerness, his eyes, the fire burning in there.
>
> Apparently he was working on the side with one of those military teams and got killed in some operation. . . . All of a sudden a lot of people were dead before I knew when or how.

One theory held by U.S. and Salvadoran sources is that Alvarez was killed for talking too much. A brief investigation by an embassy official, reported in a December 1981 cable, said that in late September, while Alvarez was watching a match between the Almacenes Pacifico soccer team and another club, a group of men thought to be plainclothes police officers hustled him out of the crowd, threw him to the ground and shot him. An item in a

San Salvador newspaper dated September 28, 1981, reports that municipal authorities found Alvarez's bullet-riddled body on a road in the capital. It said further details were lacking.

At the House hearings earlier this year, former Ambassador White charged that the State Department had cables from an eye-witness source (Killer) linking d'Aubuisson to the Romero assassination, and accused the Reagan Administration of covering up in the information. The State Department then announced that the source was dead. But when White checked with his sources in El Salvador he learned that the department's statement was false, and he said he gave Killer's real name to the Federal Bureau of Investigation.

Although there are differing accounts within the intelligence community, the preponderance of the evidence indicates that Archbishop Romero's killing sprung out of a tightly woven conspiracy involving military officers, guns for hire and wealthy civilians: the traditional Salvadoran confraternity that has always acted above the law. Yet despite Duarte's high-sounding resolve to bring to justice those responsible for the crime, a resolution of the case appears doubtful. The president's commission has no authority to act on its findings, which must be turned over to the attorney general, a member of d'Aubuisson's Arena Party. And, observed former Ambassador Rivas-Gallont, even in the best of circumstances "to convict someone in a murder case in El Salvador there needs to be a witness who saw you pull the trigger, saw the bullet hit the guy and then watched the victim fall down and bleed to death. This is difficult in a normal murder case—imagine this one!"

It does not appear that the Salvadorans will receive much help from the United States on this one. The official U.S. line on the assassination is to treat it as an internal Salvadoran affair. "We won't touch it with anything," explained an embassy source in El Salvador. "There is no U.S. support for it. If the Salvadoran government asks for confidential [cable] traffic, it will be difficult for us to cooperate because we won't disclose our sources."

The State Department's reluctance to tackle d'Aubuisson on the Romero case has at least been consistent. The Foreign Service officer who unearthed many of the details about the killing was ordered to stop his investigations shortly after his discovery of Musa, according to department sources. They said it was too dangerous. In the spring of 1982, when a Congressional committee holding hearings on the suitability of granting d'Aubuisson a visa requested all the department's files on the rightist leader, the cables linking him to the Romero assassination were withheld. Now, in the interest of not upsetting volatile right-wing forces in the Salvadoran government, the State Department is opposed to making public any conclusion in the Senate's report linking d'Aubuisson to the death squads.

From the point of view of day-to-day policy, appeasement of the violent right-wing faction headed by d'Aubuisson may seem logical, at least until other democratic forces are strengthened. But this is the logic of desperation. Four years ago, d'Aubuisson allegedly tried to seize power by throwing over the card table in the middle of the game—assassinating the highest-ranking church official in the land. Four months ago, U.S. intelligence sources learned that a group of people tied to d'Aubuisson was going to try it again—attempting to kill U.S. Ambassador Pickering and possibly President Duarte. Assassination teams were formed, guns were collected, overt actions were taken in furtherance of that plan. The plot was foiled by some fortunate tips and the persuasive power of the U.S. government. Next time we may not be so lucky.

Journey Through Morazan; the Lost People of La Joya

Jon Lee Anderson and Lucia Annunziata

In the rebel-controlled zone of northern Morazan province, El Salvador, is La Joya, home to survivors of a massacre that took place there in 1981. The "lost people" of La Joya are dramatic examples of the effect of war on civilian populations, according to the writers of the following viewpoint. The government of El Salvador considers this region controlled by guerrillas of the Farabundo Marti National Liberation Front (F.M.L.N.), and maintains that the civilians left in the area are guerrilla supporters. The authors, however, uncovered a more complex story. Jon Lee Anderson, a biographer, author, and international investigative reporter, is currently a staff writer for the New Yorker. *Lucia Annunziata, an Italian journalist and a former president of the Italian public broadcasting company RAI, is currently a writer for* La Stampa *and the* Washington Post.

> *Five years after a massacre, a Salvadoran town still battles for survival against US-backed military forces. A 1981 massacre devastated the small village of La Joya in El Salvador. Five years*

later, reporters find La Joya's residents are still being targeted by the army.

La Joya is a place that does not officially exist. It is a hamlet in the rebel-controlled zone of northern Morazan province, El Salvador. About 200 people live there, amid a patchwork of dying cornfields, mescal cactus and the remains of several strafed and bombed farmhouses. They are survivors of a massacre. On December 11, 1981, the U.S.-trained Atlacatl Battalion entered the village of Mozote and some nearby hamlets, killing more than 1,000 people. The survivors fled into the forest.

Five years later they are still in hiding, haunted by the past, pursued by fears both real and imagined. They are convinced that their relatives' killers are hunting them down to make sure they will never tell the world what happened in Mozote. As proof the army wants them dead, they say they are subjected to constant aerial attacks. The story of the lost people of La Joya is the most dramatic example of the effects of the war on the civilian population of Morazan province. The Salvadoran government considers northern Morazan to be a zone controlled by leftist guerrillas of the Farabundo Marti National Liberation Front. The government maintains that the few civilians left in the area are all F.M.L.N. supporters.

Recently we spent a week traveling in Morazan, talking to the people who live there. Based on what we observed, the government view is incorrect. Indeed, as a result of the general shift in the course of the six-year war, the civilian population, which had practically abandoned the area, is returning. At the same time, the guerrillas have withdrawn some of their forces and no longer claim northern Morazan as a liberated zone. In a shaded hollow at the base of the mountains between El Salvador and Honduras, where the river called Quebrada El Mozote levels out, eight of La Joya's families live in the open air. They left their homes after the most recent bombing, on Christmas Day last year. We spoke with 27-year-old Albina del Cid, mother of seven, as she sat in a hammock strung between two trees on the river bank. She had lived there since October, she said, after the planes scored a direct hit on her house. Before that, raiding troops had burned it down several times, but she had always managed to rebuild it.

La Joya itself—what is left of it—is a forty-minute walk from the river, halfway up a bomb-scorched hill. The only sign of habitation is the wattle and daub hut that serves as the community store. The men gather there to loaf and talk, sitting on the two long wooden benches outside. An open bit of meadow under a towering tree serves as the village's plaza. After we arrived, the people still in La Joya met and chose a dozen of their members to tell us the town's story. It was the first time in five years that any of them had dared speak of the past massacre of El Mozote and the present persecution.

Amanda Martinez, 37, a mother of five, sat on a fallen tree at the edge of the grass and described how her mother, Damasa Martinez, died last July when planes strafed La Joya:

> We were in the house when we saw the planes coming, and we left because they were shooting at us. We threw ourselves under a tree, but the planes were low, and the bullets hit her. She cried to me, and I went to her and put her close to me, but she was already dying. One bullet hit her in the back and another broke her right arm.

In a raid last September, Catalina Argueta lost her husband, Leonzo Zaen, when a bomb struck the corner of their house. In October and again on Christmas Day the planes rocketed and machine-gunned the village. No one was killed, but houses were destroyed and crops burned. In November, 15-year-old Jose Cristino Sanchez went to the town of Joateca to sell some mescal rope. A woman who accompanied him brought back the news that he had been murdered by soldiers, who then dumped his body beside the road. This was not his family's first brush with tragedy. Thirty of his relatives died in the 1981 massacre. Santos

A forensic anthropologist processes human remains found in the now uninhabited village of El Mozote, El Salvador, in 1992. The remains—fifty-eight in total—include at least fifty children and a pregnant woman. © AP Images/Michael Stravato.

Torres, who lost four children in that slaughter, told us why he thinks the people of La Joya continue to be a target: "Our error, perhaps, is that we are poor and we live here."

La Joya is not the only target. In other communities we visited, the inhabitants told of similar experiences. Sometimes soldiers attack them, sometimes planes and helicopters. The aircraft drop incendiaries and contact bombs, which explode when they strike the topmost branches of trees, scattering lethal wooden shrapnel.

The raids are only one example of the government's pacification campaign in northern Morazan. To prevent civilians from feeding the guerrillas, the army limits the amount of food and supplies each person can carry into the area to what is considered sufficient for his or her needs. Malnutrition is endemic and health conditions are inferior, even by the standards of poverty-stricken rural El Salvador.

"We were born here, and here we should die" is a phrase we heard repeatedly among the people who are returning to their hometowns in northern Morazan from the refugee camps south of the Torola River, which bisects the province. From the testimony of dozens of civilians living in the nine communities we visited, it is evident that people who left the area in 1981 and 1982 are coming back. Many of them explain that in the city or in the refugee camps everything, even water, is difficult to obtain. Here they have a house, some chickens and a piece of land. Most of them had returned because, as one put it, "At the beginning we thought the war was going to end soon, but now it seems it will go on for a long time." Another group came back in 1984, hoping that the election of President Jose Napoleon Duarte would bring peace.

These people are trying to rebuild Morazan. In Perquin the school director and his wife recently reopened the school. They have asked the government to send more teachers. The children have had no schooling for five years. Now local women with only a few years' education are teaching the youngest ones how to read and write.

The people have also created town councils, elected by secret ballot. Some have been functioning for more than a year, though most of them were formed late last year. Local rebel officers say the councils are the beginning of local self-government and insist that they are independent from guerrilla organizations. Council leaders confirm this, adding that although the guerrillas had offered suggestions on how to set them up, the councils are separate from the F.M.L.N.

The civilian population regards the guerrillas with a mixture of support and suspicion. But the dominant mood is exhaustion with the war. The people resent the government for the bombings and for abandoning them. "We are not guerrillas," they say. "We are people of this land."

Several high-ranking officers of the People's Revolutionary Army (ERP), the main F.M.L.N. force in Morazan, told us the guerrillas no longer consider the area a liberated zone. The strategy of "a country within the country" has been abandoned, one commander told us. "It is dangerous for the population and impossible for us to defend," he said. "We want to expand the war throughout the country." What has caused the change of tactics is the army's increased troop strength and air support. While maintaining bases in Morazan, the F.M.L.N. has employed small mobile groups throughout the country, shifting from the classic rural guerrilla strategy to urban warfare.

The F.M.L.N. appeared to maintain a strong presence in the area we visited. The guerrillas live in camps apart from the civilians, though they move freely through the various villages. They have their own political-military commissions, their own sources of food and medicine and their own communication network. The bombings, controls on food and the army raids seem to have been ineffectual against the rebels' small and flexible organization, which does not offer a fixed target. The only fixed targets are the civilians in the villages.

A few days after completing our tour of the countryside, we interviewed the army chief of staff, Gen. Adolfo Blandon:

Q: *Are you aware that a civilian population lives in a place known as La Joya, near Mozote?*

A: Specifically, I don't know that place.

Q: *You mean to say you didn't know people lived there?*

A: How many people do you think are in that place, approximately?

Q: *About 200, old men, women, children and adults.*

A: The terrorist use many tricks. They make a concentration in a place to attract the attention of the armed forces, then they leave the people behind precisely to cause these incidents. They try to take advantage of the situation.

We asked General Blandon about the Christmas Day bombing, which took place during a ten-day truce to which the army had agreed. Blandon could find no orders to bomb La Joya or anywhere else north of the Torola River.

"I don't think there was anything on that day," he said. "There was no reason to do that. There was no objective."

A Researcher Describes How Violence Escalated in One Guatemalan Town

Robert M. Carmack

In the following viewpoint, a US researcher details his life in Guatemala in the 1970s. There, the Indian culture was under pressure from the ladinos—people whose ancestry combined indigenous and Spanish colonial. US researchers were often caught in the middle, but the author developed an admiring relationship with the new mayor—the first Indian elected mayor in two centuries. He describes his emotions as violence in the town increased, and he learned of the death of the mayor. Robert M. Carmack has taught in universities in the United States and Latin America. His specialization is political anthropology, and he has served as a consultant to the US Embassy in Guatemala.

I lived in Guatemala for two and a half years as a young man during the 1950s and became fascinated with the ancient Maya cultures, many of whose remains I saw. Later, when I entered graduate studies in anthropology, it was quite natural that I should choose the Maya cultures of Guatemala as the object of my specialized research. Specifically, I focused on the ancient

Quiché Maya kingdom that flourished in the highlands of western Guatemala when the Spaniards reached the region. At first I concentrated on the native documents that have come down to us, including the famous "bible of the Quichés," *Popol Vuh*. Later I returned to the western highlands to carry out fieldwork among the living Quiché Indians in an isolated, traditional community. Learning the Quiché language and studying Quiché customs firsthand whetted my appetite to learn more about that remarkable culture. After all, the Quichés were the most powerful of the Maya kingdoms encountered by the Spanish conquistadors.

A logical next step was to work at the ancient capital of the Quiché kingdom, which I had visited only briefly before 1970. The old capital, now a community named Santa Cruz del Quiché (Saint Cross of the Quichés), had become a departmental center and the residence of more than thirty thousand Quiché-speaking Indians. About two miles outside town the ruins of the ancient site are witness to the past grandeur of these Indians. In neighboring Chichicastenango, the Quiché Indians burn incense in front of the church and participate in markets bursting with native crafts. Santa Cruz is greatly overshadowed by Chichicastenango, and its present-day Indian culture and ancient ruins are virtually unstudied. Thus it is scarcely possible to exaggerate the excitement my colleagues and I in the State University of New York at Albany (SUNYA) felt as we initiated a long-term project to study the Quichés of Santa Cruz. For the next ten years (1970–80) we investigated their language, customs, history, and archaeological remains.

When we came onto the scene early in the 1970s, Santa Cruz had long ceased to be a sleepy village. The department governor and other bureaucrats lived there, as did the officers and soldiers of an important military base. Spanish priests who administered the affairs of the Catholic church in the region had their headquarters in Santa Cruz. The town was also a market and transportation center for the entire region. Its many general-merchandise stores provided manufactured goods for the region, and its large bus terminal was crowded with buses coming and going at all hours of the day.

Santa Cruz of the 1970s was in the middle of a population boom; in thirty years its population had more than doubled. As compared with other townships of the region, the town center had become unusually large, with about eight thousand persons (about 23 percent of the total population) residing there. More than half of the townspeople were ladinos, who owned stores and buses or provided services for the departmental government, the army, the church, and various commercial establishments. Some Indians lived in town and performed administrative and commercial tasks, although most were simple wage earners. The rural people, 77 percent of the population and almost all Indian, scratched out an existence on lands that were capable of supporting only about one-third of the population. Large numbers of them migrated to the coast a few months each year to work on plantations. Others manufactured hats by weaving together palm fronds, the major cottage industry of Santa Cruz.

Social life in Santa Cruz was boiling over with division and conflict. The struggling factions divided Indians against ladinos, Catholics against Protestants, town against country, rich against poor. In town Protestant sects competed with one another and with the Catholics for "souls," and these religious lines tended to overlap with competing political parties. In the countryside the Catholics had launched a large-scale catechist movement, known as Catholic Action. It split the Indian peasants into traditional and modern (catechist) factions. And because the modern faction gravitated toward the Christian Democratic party, political and religious lines were intertwined in the rural area. Rural development programs followed similar cleavages, the cooperatives, water projects, and agricultural programs tending to favor the progressive catechists. By far the deepest split in Santa Cruz, however, was that between Indians and ladinos. The town ladinos controlled the most lucrative stores and bus lines, dominated the government posts, and found ways to exploit the labor and goods of the rural Indians. Widespread mutual mistrust and hostility prevailed between the ladinos and Indians, though the hostility was submerged, and social life seemed peaceful.

The Old Culture Was Hard to Find

Very little of the old Quiché culture remained at Santa Cruz. Town rituals having been "purified," the saint processions were largely devoid of native symbols. No council of elders oversaw the protection of ancient ways. The one native town official, the "Indian alcalde" (mayor), was subject to the municipal alcalde. Those aspects of traditional culture that persisted in the rural area were no longer associated with traditional clans and hamlets that had once existed. Practicing shamans could be found, the Quiché language was widely spoken, and the old altars, including the ancient ruins, were used sporadically for burning incense to the ancestors. Nevertheless, the traditional way of life, although still an option in rural Santa Cruz, was marginal.

As we learned to our disappointment, Santa Cruz residents showed little interest in the ancient Quiché culture. The old capital site lay ruined and neglected, its glorious past forgotten by all, even those most directly descended from its ancient occupants. The growing numbers of modernizing Indians, whether in town or in country, were leaving the Quiché culture behind. The ladinos viewed it either as a source of profit—through tourism or the looting of mounds—or as a symbol of their domination of the Indians. The shamans and marginal peasants still found meaning in the ancient ways, but even for them the traditions represented only a "culture of refuge," a means that the most conservative of them used to retain a semblance of community identity in the face of modernizing forces. It was a struggle of attrition; each year more ancient patterns were being rejected by new recruits of change.

This was the Santa Cruz we found in the early 1970s. We knew that research there would be difficult—just how difficult we could not have predicted—but the opportunity to study one of the great Indian civilizations of the Americas seemed to us worth the challenge.

It soon became clear that the schism between ladinos and Indians would be a source of recurrent problems for us. The rural Indians, deeply suspicious after years of exploitation by ladinos, extended their suspicions to us. One elderly Indian woman would not allow us to excavate the large archaeological mounds on her property; an Indian man in a nearby town stuck a pistol in my face when I tried to gain access to his lands to examine mounds there. To make matters worse, the Spanish priests did not trust us, and they communicated this distrust to the catechists throughout the countryside.

Our problems with the town ladinos, much more serious, were never resolved. Many "middle class" ladinos, however, were friendly. Among these was the alcalde, a local storekeeper who as a young man had traveled widely throughout Mexico and had even worked as a bracero [laborer] in the United States. But the ladino elites saw us as a definite threat to their domination of the rural Indians and the community as a whole. Broadcasts on the local Radio Quiché began accusing us of coming to rob Santa Cruz of the riches buried in its ancient sites. Gossip ran rampant through the town, and committees of concerned citizens began to obstruct our work. We traced the broadcasts to a sergeant at the local military base, but conversations with him made it apparent that he was only the agent of powerful ladinos in town.

The Indian merchants living in town saw us less as a threat than as an opportunity for exploitation. Some of them who owned lands on which ruins stood began demanding exorbitant fees from us in exchange for permission to excavate their lands. It was clear that they were digging for artifacts to be sold on the black market; a few had purchased the lands specifically to "farm" them for artifacts. Our appeals to their Indian identity were in vain; they were interested only in the money that could be earned from their property. Many of the rural Indians,

Quiché women participate in a 2001 ceremony for the victims of a 1980s massacre found in a mass grave in Zacualpa, Guatemala. © Andrea Nieto/Getty Images.

by contrast, became genuinely interested in our studies and what could be learned about the ancient Quiché culture. A few town Indians, more "middle class" than the merchants, also took a genuine interest in our work and the Quiché culture. Some of them had organized a study club, and we were invited to speak at their meetings from time to time.

An Elite Leader Keeps a Pistol

Attacks from elite ladinos were relentless throughout the years. Evidence suggested that the leader of the ladino opposition was a wealthy lawyer who controlled important businesses in town. A congressman of the Conservative party, he eventually rose to national leadership. I visited him several times, but he would never admit that he was working against us. He was a tall, handsome man with reactionary ideas. Because he shared the deep-seated ladino prejudices against the Indians, they hated him. He had other enemies as well. Consequently he kept a small cadre of bodyguards outside his office and a pistol on his table. Toward the end of our studies in Santa Cruz, when we discovered some spectacular gold pieces in the ruins, he informed the president of Guatemala that we were robbing the "national patrimony." His accusations against us and our university reached the nation's leading newspapers. At that time we turned to the other congressman from Santa Cruz, a Christian Democrat who placed the best interests of Santa Cruz above his own. I was struck by his Anglo name, Hamilton Noriega, and by his kind, understanding consideration of our problem. The contrast between the two congressmen symbolized well the contradictions that so badly fragmented the community.

One reason we did not retreat in the face of so many problems was that the ladino alcalde stayed by our side. In Guatemala, however, alcaldes cannot succeed themselves. A new alcalde was elected in 1978, the same year in which Gen. Lucas García became president of Guatemala. The results of the election filled us with renewed hope. The new alcalde, Andrés Avelino Zapeta y Zapeta, was the first Indian elected in Santa Cruz for perhaps two hundred years. Furthermore, he seemed to represent a link between town and country, ladinos and Indians. He worked as a carpenter in a hamlet on the outskirts of town and was a leader in the catechist movement. He was a kind, gentle man, neither cynical about the future (like some peasants) nor indifferent to Quiché culture (like many town Indians). He was proud of his Indian heritage, and he offered to help us learn about the ancient ways, which, he said, were "the true history of Guatemala." With Alcalde Zapeta at the helm, things were looking up for us and for Santa Cruz.

By 1979, however, when we tried to expand our work at Santa Cruz, all was not well in Guatemala. It had been widely reported in both Guatemalan and foreign newspapers that the army had massacred more than one hundred Kekchí Indians at Panzós in May 1978. Guerrillas were known to be operating among the Ixil Indians living in the mountainous northern part of El Quiché Department.

I was personally quite conscious of the escalation of violence after the 1978 election of General Lucas García. I wrote in my diary that year: "Revolution is at the door; people are so tired of problems that none will defend the government. Only the army defends, and it has become a privileged elite, selfish and unpopular." Still I considered the violence simply a part of the conflict that had long characterized Guatemalan social life. Not wanting to believe that the situation was as serious as it really was, I allowed myself to be persuaded by voices of moderation. The director of the USAID mission in Guatemala, a man I admired, spoke of U.S. efforts to support the poor. The governor of Quiché, an army officer, claimed that the guerrillas were restricted to the northern area and were not succeeding. A Protestant minister from Santa Cruz who traveled extensively throughout the Quiché region told me that the guerrillas had failed to win over the Indians, although they did have a few supporters in the northern mountainous zone.

The Danger Kept Growing

In 1980 we won another grant to continue work at Santa Cruz. But, growing nervous for the safety of my colleagues and me at Santa Cruz, I determined to discover whether or not guerrilla activity actually existed in the community. I was shown leaflets containing death threats against persons in Santa Cruz. The leaflets, I was told, had been delivered by masked men armed with machine guns. Other death threats had been painted on walls. The townspeople claimed that the latter threats had been painted by army soldiers early one morning. The consensus seemed to be that there were a few guerrillas in the area but that the real action was in the north.

The situation at Santa Cruz continued to deteriorate. Soon it became obvious that it was dangerous for us to work there any longer. Indian friends of ours living near the ancient ruins—actual descendants of the Quiché kings—told us about the murder of an Indian, a cooperative leader, that they had witnessed directly in front of the ruins. Our friends said that the army appeared to have done the killing. Alcalde Zapeta also admitted that murders were occurring in Santa Cruz, although he believed that the guerrillas were committing atrocities as bad as those of the army.

In June 1980, the guerrillas ordered all Americans to leave the Quiché Department. Some archaeologists from our project who were overseeing the preservation of artifacts recovered during excavations beat a hasty retreat.

In July, after one priest had been assassinated and his own life threatened, the Spanish bishop ordered his priests to abandon the diocese. In September I decided to return to Santa Cruz for one last visit, mainly to bid farewell to Alcalde Zapeta, our good friend and supporter. I found a very tense town. Several friends came up to me and whispered that it was dangerous for me to be there, that I should leave at once. I stayed long enough to have a final interview with the alcalde. What I learned in that meeting and afterward I recorded in my diary when I had returned to the safety of my hotel in Guatemala City. . . .

The Diary Describes a Special Man

September 24, 1980

I write at this moment because I want to capture the heartache and the outrage that I feel. I just learned that yesterday the mayor of Santa Cruz Quiché, a rural town in the mountains of Guatemala, was assassinated by a band of gunmen. Perhaps his death is nothing special, for several thousand Guatemalans have been assassinated for political reasons in the past few years. But I knew this man, even more, I had a long and warm conversation with him the very morning before his tragic death. I want his people to know who he was, and why he died, because I do not want his death to be in vain. Perhaps his story can help us understand what is happening in this tiny Central American country, and what might be done someday to change the course of events there. . . .

The ladinos considered Zapeta incompetent for the post [of mayor], and, indeed, he was not prepared for the exquisite machinations that characterize town politics even in an obscure, small town such as Santa Cruz. It was obvious to the observer that Spanish was not Zapeta's native language, a fatal flaw in a culture that places great stock in oratory agility. His rural background had not prepared him for the kinds of problems he would have to confront in town: finding sufficient sources of potable water, constructing paved roads in and around town, striking a balance between serving the ladinos and helping the Indians, dealing with "development" agents from the City, dampening the quarrels between members of his own town council, and many others.

The characteristic that probably represented Zapeta's greatest liability was his deep religious convictions. Despite the fact that Guatemala is a Catholic country, and most people in Santa Cruz hold religious beliefs (agnosticism is virtually unthinkable), political life is highly secular. Zapeta's simple beliefs ill-prepared him for the elaborate struggles for power and wealth that give form to politics in towns like Santa Cruz.

But I found in Zapeta much to admire, and I loved him. He reminded me of my own father in some basic way. He was refreshingly open—innocent—about the centuries-long conflict between Indians and ladinos. Even in that last conversation he repeated again the story of how his mother and father had warned him about the ladinos, and how they would try to keep the Indians from progressing. This was said in the presence of my ladino companion, a government official from the City, a gesture of courage very rarely exhibited in this country.

Zapeta was proud to be an Indian, and said so openly. Most Indians of Santa Cruz try to hide the fact, hoping thereby to avoid in some small way the scornful discrimination heaped on them by a ladino-dominated society. Zapeta was like a child who had discovered a new world in school; he had determined that his native culture was, after all, one of dignity and worth.

Each time I saw him he would recall the beliefs and practices of his parents and forefathers, and would moralize about how the old ways should not be lost as the Indians take on new ways. I always felt certain that these lectures were exactly the ones he gave to his own family and to the many peasant Indians who visited his mayor's office to seek advice and counsel.

Zapeta was a carpenter and farmer. He worked with his sons in a humble shop attached to his house. I can imagine that his skills, and even his tools, were not too different from those applied by Jesus of Nazareth. Zapeta's economic conditions seemed to have led him to deep religious convictions. He was attracted to a progressive Catholic movement sweeping Guatemala in the 1950s and 1960s, which in many ways stood in relation to traditional Catholicism as did the Puritan reforms of 16th- and 17th-century Europe. Under the direction of European priests, the movement had some social and political goals—land reform, free elections, honesty in government—but in Santa Cruz it mainly consisted of simplifying the Church sacraments, and living a good life. Zapeta became a catechist and leader in the movement, but as best as I could tell, he never assimilated the secular goals.

It would require a long and complicated account to describe the political conditions that brought Zapeta into office, and that have risen like a dark storm since then. To put it as succinctly as possible, forces have been unleashed in Guatemala from both the extreme right and left that have destroyed all middle positions. Even a town as isolated and economically insignificant as Santa Cruz had fallen prey to those forces. That very day, yesterday as I write this, Zapeta had told me in plain and simple language what was happening in his town. In one hamlet the Catholics had been harassed and several of them killed by government soldiers, and some had now taken up arms. They had attacked an army patrol on maneuvers nearby, and apparently had joined with guerrilla bands operating in the area. Zapeta was totally opposed to this, and had told them so. "Where in the Bible does it say we should kill?" he had asked them.

That morning when we visited Zapeta, his melancholy was apparent, but he was happy because he was about to take two weeks' leave from his mayor's job to work at his home. I thought, as I left him, of the sacrifice it was for Zapeta to serve as mayor. To be devoid of political ambitions, and worse, political understanding, and yet to suffer the recriminations from former brothers and the hated ladinos alike. This was too heavy a sacrifice to make. His love of church, family, Indian culture, work, and virtue seemed so out of place in the world in which Guatemala was now living.

The radio report was simple: "Avelino Zapeta, mayor of Santa Cruz Quiché, was ambushed and assassinated by an armed band as he walked to his fields to hoe his maize plants. The identity of the assassins is unknown."

Summary of Genocide Proceedings Before the Spanish Federal Court; Round One, February 4–8, 2008

Kate Doyle

In 2008 the Spanish National Court heard testimony from surviving victims of the Guatemalan genocide. In the following viewpoint, a Mayan man tells how his family was massacred and his home destroyed by Guatemalan soldiers. Another man testifies that soldiers came to his peaceful aldea, *or village, when he was ten years old and committed rapes and slaughter, including the murder of his two-year-old brother. Kate Doyle is a senior analyst at George Washington University's National Security Archive and director of its Guatemala Documentation Project. She attended the court hearings as an observer.*

Juan Manual Jerónimo, survivor of the Plan de Sánchez massacre, was the third witness of the day. On July 18, 1982, he and his family were with his mother when someone came running to the house to warn them that the Army was coming. His mother urged him and his brother-in-law to flee and not to worry about the women or the children: "You are the ones they are looking for, not us!" They left the *aldea* but hid nearby and heard much of what happened as the soldiers attacked. When they returned the next day, Jerónimo found his family's bodies in the home of one of his brothers. They were all there: his wife, four children, siblings, aunts and uncles, cousins, and mother. They were 18 of the 184 people who died in the massacre.

Jerónimo and his brother-in-law buried the bodies of their relatives and fled. He told Judge Pedraz, "We couldn't rest anywhere for thinking about our dead. When I thought of my house, I imagined my family there. It caused me tremendous pain. The soldiers killed them. They took our animals. They cooked our chickens right there and ate them, without shame, as though they were the owners of our things. When they had stolen everything they wanted, they burned our houses, including our clothes and our land documents." The witness remained in the mountains for the next three years, "but we never went far. We didn't want to leave our dear ones who died in our village."

When the witness had finished, one of the assistant lawyers asked him if in the years leading up to the massacre and after he returned in the amnesty of 1984, the military had placed any prohibitions on the Mayan way of life. Jerónimo said yes, "They prohibited everything connected to our culture. They didn't allow us to wear our *traje* (traditional clothing), they prevented our religious customs. We weren't allowed to gather, make sacrifices and pray. Our mother language was Achí, but they no longer permitted us to talk in this dialect."

The final witness to testify before Judge Pedraz was Jesús Tecu Osorio. Tecu was a child when the military began attacking the communities of Rabinal with increasing intensity during 1981 and into 1982. By the end of 1981, many people had moved into his village of Río Negro because of massacres in the zone. They came seeking refuge. The Army and the civil patrol (PAC) of nearby Xococ ordered the people to organize a PAC in Río Negro, and told them it was obligatory to capture and kill local men suspected of subversion—but the Rio Negro PAC never did that, Tecu said, unlike PACs in other areas. This angered the military.

A mural in Plan de Sanchez, Guatemala, depicts the 1982 massacre by the Guatemalan Army.
© AP Images/Rodrigo Abd.

In February 1982, Tecu's parents were disappeared when they reported to the nearby base as ordered to obtain his father's military ID card (*cedula*). One month later, on March 13, 1982, the Army and Xococ patrollers arrived in Río Negro. Tecu recounted how they removed the women and children from their houses and forced them to climb for several hours up the hill beyond the *aldea*. The men were kept in the village and killed. Tecu, who was 10 years old, went with the women and carried his two-year-old brother during the climb.

The troops hit the children during the climb, abusing them, saying that their parents were with the guerrillas. When they came to a stop, the men raped the women there. "The people of Río Negro were completely surrounded by the soldiers and patrollers," remembered Tecu. The troops began to kill the women. They shot some of them and strangled others and threw the bodies in the ravine. Tecu tried to withdraw with his baby brother to run away, but there were too many soldiers. By that afternoon, they finished the killing. Seventeen children remained alive. One civil patroller from Xococ, Pedro González Gómez, told Tecu that he was going to Xococ because Gónzalez didn't have children and he wanted to give Tecu to his wife. He refused to take Tecu's brother, however, and so took the child from Tecu's arms and smashed him against some rocks. When he was dead he threw him down in the ravine with the rest of the corpses.

Tecu survived as a prisoner of González Gómez—first with the Xococ patrol, and later in his home. He was freed in 1983. Under questioning after he completed his testimony, he told the judge that Pedro González Gómez was convicted to the death penalty for his crimes in 1999. But Tecu pointed out that the December 2007 decision of Guatemala's Constitutional Court not to extradite senior military and police officers for the same crimes shows that "the government is willing to condemn an indigenous to the death penalty, but no one dares do that to the intellectual authors of the genocide. For that reason, we came to Spain."

A Guatemalan Soldier Relates His Shock at Tactics Used on Prisoners

Victor Montejo

In the following viewpoint, a former member of the Guatemalan military, Chilin Hultaxh, explains to a scholar how he learned what was really going on during the nation's genocidal period. Hultaxh joined the army out of financial necessity and was assigned to an office job because he had completed the equivalent of high school. He did not expect to see the terror he experienced firsthand and certainly not to be a participant. Later, he did not know how to escape. Victor Montejo is a professor of Native American Studies at the University of California, Davis, and the author of five books; from 2004 to 2008 he was a member of the Congress of Guatemala.

W ell, I want to give you a rundown of the situation I experienced in Quiché and later in Huehuetenango. It was painful for me who came from a school where I was taught very high moral principles, mostly Christian, where I learned to respect the life of my fellow humans, modesty, serving others, responsibility, which maybe at the time I never fully realized. But the army was aware of my capabilities at work and knew my professional work ethic. Gradually they isolated me from the other specialized workers because I had no experience yet in the specialized troops. When the team of specialized troops was all complete in the personnel department, I was already in Huehuetenango; they told me that they had no vacancy left for me and that there was work for me only in the intelligence section. As soon as my friends heard that I was transferring to the intelligence department, they started calling me "Spy, spy, murderer, assassin!" They knew from experience what type of work I would have to do in intelligence. I didn't pay any attention to them, it was part of army life, but at times we were very hard on each other. When I started in the intelligence section, I found a friend right away; I'll call him a friend because he respected me enough, and showed me respect and appreciation in the army. Maybe it was a psychological scheme to pull me down into the quagmire they were in. This man treated me in a very friendly manner and started to teach me how to do the periodic briefing papers for operations, for intelligence, the statistics, the messages, the official memos, and other documents that had to do with the intelligence section.

Let me at this point explain why I mentioned my simple and humble family background. My parents are peasants. Those are my roots. I grew up with the Catholic religion. This background creates a strong sense in a person to respect others. In the intelligence section I was given access to the general archive. I began to see wounded men in the office. I began to see bloody uniforms, dead bodies, even bodies of special troops who'd been killed in combat or ambushed by guerrilla forces. I saw friends, indigenous persons who'd been killed after being captured by the military. Even though this made me sad, I told myself: I can take this, no problem, it'll pass soon. I was very surprised when one time, after I'd seen all these things for a while, the friend I mentioned before called me and told me a lot about the work of the intelligence troops; until then I had only performed typing jobs.

I was never on the inside of groups like the Escuadrón de la Muerte [Death Squad], Mano Blanca [White Hand], or G-2. They had many names. The OSA or the ESA—it's all the same. It's an invention of the military leaders. They give different names to these groups, as the friend explained; these groups are made up of all the many civilians who help the army. But this is a lie. They're the very same soldiers who pass themselves off as different groups so that they can carry out the heinous crimes they committed in Guatemala.

Visiting the Prisoners

I want to tell you this friend's name. It was Lito A. Santay. He was from Palmar and has since been killed by the guerrillas. He once invited me to go and look at some "prisoners of war," as he called them. I went with him. "Take a pencil and paper, you'll need to write down information on some of the men," he told me. There were sixteen young men from Parraxtut, from the municipality of Nebaj in Quiché. They had been captured the third week in April, and on April 28 the army started to execute them extra-judicially, without court trials, in their own installations in the military zone. But I'm going too fast. When I went that day to see these boys, they lay stretched out, face down, one hand of one man tied to one hand of the next man. I started to ask them their names. They looked very normal, but you could read the fear in their faces and sense the terror they felt. Behind me were several armed military men of the Policía Militar Ambulante [Mobile Military Police]. Being from the specialized troop, I went to the captives asking their names, even joked with them. "They'll surely let you go, I just need to take down some information," I told them, really not knowing what the army had planned for them. Then we left and Lito said, "The boys need to get some food." The nice, kind tone of voice in which Lito said this made me believe that the prisoners were going to be set free. We brought them food, and they were fed well.

Four days later I was called and told, "Look, we have a job to do and want you there with us." "With pleasure," I replied. Military orders were never questioned. I had to be there. They called me. . . . They had five young men tied up.

The military execution ground in Huehuetenango has two enclosed cells, three men were in the one on one side, two in the other. They picked them up from the ammunition storerooms where they had been kept prisoner and took them to the execution ground. On the way they told them, "Well, we'll let you go. Get ready because you'll go home. We just want you in here for a little while."

But they lied to them. The torturers prepared some ropes and lassos while the prisoners waited inside. Then they called the first one. These captives had their hands tied behind their backs. They told him, "Get down on your face." The young man obeyed, knelt down, and lowered his head while Lito said, "You're a guerrillero, son of a bitch, you better tell us where your friends are, where the other guerrilleros are, or you'll see what happens."

"I know nothing," said the boy, "I know nothing, Mister. If I did, I'd already have told you."

"Shut up, then," they said, and at that moment Lito put a rope around the peasant's neck and with a stick tightened it and throttled him till he was dead. This was the first shock I got. I was shaking. I wanted to defend this man but couldn't. Very close to me stood a captain by the name of P. Pérez, a native from Tecún Umán, San Marcos. He was armed. So was Lito. And there were two other policemen. I was the only one there without a weapon. They then called the other prisoner and killed him, too. They killed all five young men, one by one.

Lito asked me, "You want to try one?" I couldn't take it any longer and started to vomit. "No!" I said. "I can't stand it. I can't do this." I still saw before my eyes the man's face when they strangled him and heard the poor guy say, "Oh God, oh God," when the soldiers started to kill him. Foam and blood came out of his mouth. I couldn't stop shaking and had to vomit

Trapped Amid the Dead

"Get a grip on yourself!" the captain told me. "Okay, I will, Captain," I said. While these men were killed, the captives who were inside were not aware of what was going on. The dead were left under a tarp. I even helped drag their poor bodies there under the tarp. I was ordered to help put the bodies into a truck. Without any clothes or IDs, the victims' bodies were put into that truck—which was metallic gray. It was about 11:00 P.M., and they took them away to an unknown destination. Later Lito told me they had to kill the sixteen young men because they were people who for sure would have joined the guerrilla troops. The young men had been caught when the army soldiers had disguised themselves as guerrilleros and had held a "guerrilla" meeting. That's how these friends had been trapped. Their bodies were thrown out of the truck at the highway kilometer marker 313 near Boquerón, where the Pan-American Highway passes by coming from Mesilla. Many of our fellow countrymen were thrown there. Many people who belonged or who did not belong to guerrilla groups were dumped there by the military. This hit me the hardest of all. From this moment on I could not sleep anymore. I knew then what was in store for me. I had to decide whether I wanted to stay in the army. If I got blood on my hands, I'd come out the loser. From then on I tried to get drunk frequently in order to make mistakes so they'd kick me out of the army, for I was afraid to ask for a discharge because if they granted it, they might want to kill me.

Glossary

ARENA The governing right-wing party in El Salvador for much of the civil war. Its full name in English is the Nationalist Republican Alliance; in Spanish, Alianza Republicana Nacionalista.

campesinos A Spanish word meaning small-scale farmers, farm workers, or peasants.

CEH The Spanish abbreviation for the Guatemalan Commission for Historical Clarification, which concluded that the military government committed genocide in the national conflict.

FAES The armed forces of El Salvador.

finca A Spanish word for a substantial rural property—usually a large farm, ranch, plantation, or estate.

FMLN The main guerrilla coalition that opposed the right-wing government in El Salvador. The organization was named for the leader of the 1932 peasant rebellion; in English the group is Farabundo Martí National Liberation Front and in Spanish, Frente Farabundo Martí para la Liberación Nacional.

FSLN The Sandinista party; Frente Sandinista de Liberación Nacional.

GOG Government of Guatemala

indio A Spanish word meaning Indian, indigenous person, or Native American.

junta A small group of military and/or political leaders who forcibly take over a country.

ladino A person whose ancestry is both Spanish and Central American Indian.

matazonas Areas within Guatemala that the military declared were killing zones. In such areas, civilians (including children) as well as insurgents were subject to lethal force.

Sandinista The Sandinistas began as a left-wing rebel group in Nicaragua. Leaders of the Sandinista movement were elected as Nicaragua's government in 1979, and it continues as a prominent political party.

URNG The largest group opposing repression by the Guatemalan government forces. Its name in English is the Guatemalan National Revolutionary Unity; in Spanish, Unidad Revolucionaria Nacional Guatemalteca.

Organizations to Contact

The editors have compiled the following list of organizations concerned with the issues debated in this book. The descriptions are derived from materials provided by the organizations. All have publications or information available for interested readers. The list was compiled on the date of publication of the present volume; the information provided here may change. Be aware that many organizations take several weeks or longer to respond to inquiries, so allow as much time as possible.

Amnesty International
5 Penn Plaza
New York, NY 10001
(212) 807-8400 • fax: (212) 627-1451
e-mail: aimember@aiusa.org
website: www.amnestyusa.org

Amnesty International opposes injustice and promotes human rights in more than 150 countries. The organization mobilizes citizens to press governments to uphold the Universal Declaration of Human Rights. The organization frequently posts research and policy reports on its website and publishes a newsletter for members.

Center for Justice and Accountability
870 Market Street, Suite 680
San Francisco, CA 94102
(415) 544-0444 • fax: (415) 544-0456
e-mail: center4justice@cja.org
website: http://cia.org

The center aims to deter torture and other extreme human rights abuses around the world while supporting the rights of survivors to obtain truth, justice, and redress. The group pursues what it calls a survivor-centered prosecution of human rights abusers. The center's website posts the status of the group's various cases, which include special attention to Latin America.

Freedom House
1301 Connecticut Ave. NW, Floor 6
Washington, DC 20036
(202) 296-5101 • fax: (202) 526-4611
e-mail: info@freedomhouse.org
website: www.freedomhouse.org

With a history of bipartisan opposition to totalitarianism, Freedom House promotes democracy through advocacy. It has offices in a dozen countries and partners with activists to support women's rights, justice for torture victims, free speech, and human rights overall. Its best-known publication is *Freedom in the World*, an annual survey of political rights and civil liberties worldwide, and it surveys press freedom, post-Communist situations, and governance in sixty countries.

Guatemala Human Rights Commission/USA
3321 12th Street NE
Washington, DC 20017
(202) 529-6599 • fax: (202) 526-4611
e-mail: ghrc-usa@ghrc-usa.org
website: www.ghrc-usa.org

This nonpartisan humanitarian organization reports on the status of human rights in Guatemala, speaks up for abuse survivors, and works for systemic improvements. Its main activities include educational outreach, advocating to government officials, and providing aid to abuse victims. The commission publishes a newsletter called *El Quetzal* and provides news of its activities on its website.

Human Rights Watch
350 Fifth Ave., 34th Floor
New York, NY 10118

(212) 290-4700 • fax: (212) 736-1300
e-mail: hrwpress@hrw.org
website: www.hrw.org

This organization defends and protects human rights around the world. It draws international attention to rights abuses, investigates questionable situations, and organizes targeted advocacy on legal and moral grounds. Human Rights Watch frequently publishes reports on human rights violations.

Institute for Global Labour and Human Rights
5 Gateway Center, 6th Floor
Pittsburgh, PA 15222
(412) 562-2406 • fax: (412) 562-2411
e-mail: inbox@glhr.org
website: www.globallabourrights.org

The institute defends and promotes human, women's, and workers' rights in the global economy. Through research, reports, and public campaigns, the organization focuses on supporting exploited workers. Topical reports appear on its website about once a month.

Joan B. Kroc Institute for Peace and Justice
5998 Alcala Park
San Diego, CA 92110
(619) 260-4600 • fax: (619) 260-6820
e-mail: peacestudies@sandiego.edu
website: www.sandiego.edu/peacestudies/ipj

The institute, which is affiliated with the University of San Diego and the Joan B. Kroc School of Peace Studies, draws upon Catholic social teaching and sees peace and justice as inseparable. It offers programs in human rights and conflict resolution that promote scholarship and action. The institute publishes a blog, newsletter, conference reports, lecture booklets, and policy briefs, all available through its website.

Montreal Institute for Genocide and Human Rights Studies
Concordia University
1455 De Maisonneuve Blvd. West
Montreal, Quebec, H3G 1M8 Canada
(514) 848-2424 ext. 5729 or 2404 • fax: (514) 848-4538
website: http://migs.concordia.ca

MIGS, founded in 1986, monitors native language media for early warning signs of genocide in countries deemed to be at risk of mass atrocities. The institute houses the Will to Intervene (W2I) Project, a research initiative focused on the prevention of genocide and other mass atrocity crimes. The institute also collects and disseminates research on the historical origins of mass killings and provides comprehensive links to this and other research materials on its website. The website also provides numerous links concerning genocide and related issues, as well as specialized sites organized by nation, region, or case.

Rapoport Center for Human Rights and Justice
University of Texas School of Law
727 E. Dean Keeton Street
Austin, TX 78705
(512) 232-4857 • fax: (512) 471-6988
e-mail: humanrights@law.utexas.edu
website: www.utexas.edu/law/centers/humanrights

With special attention to Guatemala, the center analyzes and promotes human rights and social justice. It provides a platform for activists and scholars, organizes conferences, develops research, and archives information. Its website lists its reports and related publications.

Security Sector Reform Resource Centre
57 Erb Street West
Waterloo, Ontario, Canada N2L 6C2
(519) 885-2444 ext. 261 • fax (519) 885-5450

e-mail: info@ssrresourcecentre.org
website: www.ssrresourcecentre.org

Part of the Centre for International Governance Innovation, the SSRRC monitors and publicizes justice, security, and human rights situations in selected countries, including El Salvador. It organizes forums, archives information, and provides a document database that encourages researchers to share their findings. Its website contains country profiles, links to SSR Issue Papers, and other topical resources, including videos.

STAND/United to End Genocide
1025 Connecticut Ave., Suite 310
Washington, DC 20036
(202) 556-2100
e-mail: info@standnow.org
website: www.standnow.org

STAND is the student-led division of United to End Genocide (formerly Genocide Intervention Network). STAND envisions a world in which the global community is willing and able to protect civilians from genocide and mass atrocities. In order to empower individuals and communities with the tools to prevent and stop genocide, STAND recommends activities from engaging government representatives to hosting fundraisers and has more than one thousand student chapters at colleges and high schools. While maintaining many documents online regarding genocide, STAND provides a plan to promote action as well as education.

United Human Rights Council (UHRC)
104 N. Belmont Street, Suite 313
Glendale, CA 91206
(818) 507-1933
website: www.unitedhumanrights.org

The United Human Rights Council is a committee of the Armenian Youth Federation. By means of action on a grassroots level, the UHRC works toward exposing and correcting human rights violations of governments worldwide. The UHRC campaigns against violators in an effort to generate awareness through boycotts, community outreach, and education. The UHRC website focuses on the genocides of the twentieth century.

United Nations Office of the Special Adviser for the Prevention of Genocide
866 United Nations Plaza, Suite 600
New York, NY 10017
(917) 367-2589 • fax: (917) 367-3777
e-mail: osapg@un.org
website: www.un.org/preventgenocide/adviser

This office raises awareness of the causes and dynamics of genocide and seeks to mobilize appropriate action. Working closely with the UN Security Council, the office provides expert advice, assistance, and organization to governments as well as the UN. Its website provides links to declarations, official reports, and other documents.

United States Institute of Peace's Genocide Prevention Task Force
2301 Constitution Ave. NW
Washington, DC 20037
(202) 457-1700 • fax: (202) 429-6063
e-mail: info@usip.org
website: www.usip.org/programs/initiatives/genocide
-prevention-task-force

This task force develops practical recommendations to help the US government respond to emerging threats of mass atrocities. Its staff reports and those of other experts are publicized on its website. The task force's major publication is *Preventing Genocide: A Blueprint for U.S. Policymakers*, co-chaired by Madeleine K. Albright and William S. Cohen.

List of Primary Source Documents

The editors have compiled the following list of primary source documents that either broadly address genocide and persecution or more narrowly focus on the topic of this volume. The full text of these documents is available from multiple sources in print and online.

Congressional Research Service Report on El Salvador, August 31, 2012

This report examines political and economic conditions in El Salvador in the years after the nation's civil war as well as its relationship with the United States.

Convention Against Torture and Other Cruel, Inhuman, or Degrading Punishment, United Nations, December 10, 1984

A resolution adopted by the United Nations General Assembly opposing any nation's use of torture, unusually harsh punishment, and unfair imprisonment.

Convention on the Prevention and Punishment of the Crime of Genocide, United Nations, December 9, 1948

A resolution of the United Nations General Assembly that defines genocide in legal terms and advises participating countries to prevent and punish actions of genocide in war and peacetime.

Principles of International Law Recognized in the Charter of the Nuremberg Tribunal, United Nations International Law Commission, 1950

After World War II (1939–1945), the victorious allies put surviving leaders of Nazi Germany on trial in the German city of Nuremberg. The proceedings established standards for international law that were affirmed by the United Nations and by later court tests. Among other standards, national leaders can be held responsible for crimes against humanity, which might include "murder, extermination, deportation, enslavement, and other inhuman acts."

Rome Statute of the International Criminal Court, July 17, 1998

This treaty established the International Criminal Court, including its functions, jurisdiction, and structure. In April 2012, Guatemala became the 121st nation to join the ICC system.

Stockholm Declaration on Genocide Prevention, January 28, 2004

A statement signed by fifty-five national governments declaring they "are committed to doing our utmost" to prevent genocide, mass murder, ethnic cleansing, and impunity for those who commit such acts.

Supreme Court of Spain Decision Concerning the Guatemala Genocide Case, February 25, 2003

A Guatemalan group filed a lawsuit in Spain based on the principle of universal jurisdiction that says crimes such as genocide can be prosecuted in other countries if the original country's government fails to investigate. The Supreme Court of Spain found that certain individuals should be prosecuted for the genocide in Guatemala.

United Nations General Assembly Resolution 96 on the Crime of Genocide, December 11, 1946

A resolution of the United Nations General Assembly that affirms genocide is a crime under international law.

Universal Declaration of Human Rights, United Nations, December 10, 1948

A general statement of individual rights that the United Nations hoped would apply worldwide.

Whitaker Report on Genocide, United Nations Economic and Social Council Commission on Human Rights, 1985

A report addressing the prevention of genocide. It calls for the establishment of an international criminal court and a system of universal jurisdiction to ensure that genocide is punished.

For Further Research

Books

Robert Armstrong and Janet Shenk, *El Salvador: The Face of Revolution*. Boston: South End, 1982.

Leigh Binford, *The Massacre at El Mozote: Anthropology and Human Rights*. Tucson: University of Arizona Press, 1996.

Kenneth J. Campbell, *Genocide and the Global Village*. New York: Palgrave, 2001.

Nidia Diaz, *I Was Never Alone: A Prison Diary from El Salvador*. New York: Ocean, 1992.

Paul J. Dosal, *Power in Transition: The Rise of Guatemala's Industrial Oligarchy, 1871–1994*. Westport, CT: Praeger, 1995.

Margaret Hooks, ed., *Guatemalan Women Speak*. London: Catholic Institute for International Relations, 1991.

Max G. Manwaring and Court Prisk, eds., *El Salvador at War: An Oral History of Conflict from the 1979 Insurrection to the Present*. Washington, DC: National Defense University Press, 1988.

Stephen Schlesinger and Stephen Kinzer, *Bitter Fruit: The Story of the American Coup in Guatemala*. Cambridge, MA: David Rockefeller Center Series on Latin American Studies, Harvard University, 1982.

Jean-Marie Simon, *Guatemala: Eternal Spring, Eternal Tyranny*. New York: W.W. Norton, 1987.

Jon Sobrino, *Archbishop Romero: Memories and Reflections*. Maryknoll, NY: Orbis, 1990.

Margarita S. Studemeister, ed., *El Salvador: Implementation of the Peace Accords*. Washington, DC: US Institute of Peace, 2001.

Maria Teresa Tula, *Hear My Testimony: Maria Teresa Tula, Human Rights Activist of El Salvador*. Boston: South End, 1999.

Daniel Wilkinson, *Silence on the Mountain: Stories of Terror, Betrayal and Forgetting in Guatemala*. Boston and New York: Houghton Mifflin, 2002.

Stefan Woolf, *Ethnic Conflict: A Global Perspective*. Oxford, England: Oxford University Press, 2006.

Periodicals and Internet Sources

Alison Acker, "How to Steal an Election," *Briarpatch*, June 2004.

Mike Allison, "El Salvador's Brutal Civil War: What We Still Don't Know," *Al Jazeera*, March 1, 2012. www.aljazeera.com.

Richard Amesbury and Andrew Kirschman, "Salvador's Saint: Thirty Years After His Death, Archbishop Oscar Romero Remains a Guiding Presence," *America*, April 26, 2010.

Patrick Ball, Charles R. Hale, Beatriz Manz, June Nash, Elizabeth Oglesby, Amy Ross, and Carol Smith, "Democracy as Subterfuge? Researchers Under Siege in Guatemala," *LASA Forum*, vol. 23, no. 3, 2002.

Mario Bencastro, "El Salvador's Poet of Recovery," *Americas*, March 2001.

Richard Boudreaux, "Civil War Ends in El Salvador with Signing of Treaty," *Los Angeles Times*, January 17, 1992. http://articles.latimes.com.

Audrey R. Chapman and Patrick Ball, "The Truth of Truth Commissions," *Human Rights Quarterly*, vol. 23, no. 1, 2001.

Mark Danner, "The Truth of El Mozote," *New Yorker*, December 6, 1993.

Brintnall Douglas, "The Guatemalan Indian Civil Rights Movement," *Cultural Survival Quarterly*, Spring 1983. www .culturalsurvival.org.

Kate Doyle, "Guatemala's Genocide: Survivors Speak," *NACLA Report on the Americas*, May–June 2008.

Susan Dwyer, "Reconciliation for Realists," *Ethics and International Affairs*, vol. 13, 1999.

Molly Fitzpatrick, "El Salvador: A Story of Hope and Perseverance," *UN Chronicle*, September–November 2006.

Richard J. Goldstone, "Justice as a Tool for Peace-Keeping: Truth Commissions and International Criminal Tribunals," *New York University Journal of International Law and Politics*, vol. 28, no. 3, 1996.

Alma Guillermoprieto, "In the New Gangland of El Salvador," *New York Review of Books*, November 10, 2011.

Jeff Severns Guntzel, "Maryknoll Marks 25 Years Since Martyrs' Deaths," *National Catholic Reporter*, December 16, 2005.

Edgar Gutiérrez, "Memory and Reconciliation: The Story of Guatemala," *World Association for Christian Communication*, April 2001. www.waccglobal.org.

Charles R. Hale, "Consciousness, Violence and the Politics of Memory in Guatemala," *Current Anthropology*, vol. 38, no. 5, December 1997.

Chris Herrera and Michael G. Nelson, "Salvadoran Reconciliation," *Military Review*, July–August 2008.

Indian Law Resource Center, "Guatemala Court Makes Landmark Ruling in Indigenous Rights Case," February 8, 2011. www.indianlaw.org.

Julia Preston, "Guatemala and Guerrillas Sign Accord to End 35-Year Conflict," *New York Times*, September 20, 1996. www.nytimes.com.

Scott Wallace, "You Must Go Home Again," *Harper's Magazine*, August 2000.

Lauren Wolfe, "Reckoning with a Genocide in Guatemala," *The Atlantic*, February 10, 2012. www.theatlantic.com.

Pilar Yoldi, Yolanda Aguilar, and Claudia Estrada, "Guatemala's Women During the Long War: 'Treated Worse than Animals,'" *Envio Digital*, July 1999. www.envio.org.

Websites

El Salvador: War, Peace, and Human Rights, 1980–1994 (www.gwu.edu/~nsarchiv/nsa/publications/elsalvador2/). This website provides information about the National Security Archive's collection of declassified US government records that chart Washington's participation in the conflict in El Salvador.

Guatemala (http://washlaw.edu/forint/america/guatemala .html). An annotated website maintained by the Washburn University School of Law, this resource focuses on governmental and legal aspects of Guatemala.

Guatemala Civil War 1960–1996 (www.globalsecurity.org /military/world/war/guatemala.htm). This annotated website, maintained by GlobalSecurity.org, provides a summarized history of the Guatemalan conflict, maps showing stages in the war, and further links.

Justice and the Generals (www.pbs.org/wnet/justice/elsalvador .html). This website provides a concise summary of the El Salvador civil war in addition to pictures and video illuminating the conflict.

Resources on Genocide in Guatemala (http://preventgeno cide.org/edu/pastgenocides/guatemala/resources/). This website provides a compilation of links about the genocide in Guatemala.

Film

Granito: How to Nail a Dictator (2011) This documentary traces five characters whose paths collide in wartime Guatemala.

Guazapa: Yesterday's Enemies (2010) In this documentary, war correspondent Don North shows his 1983 experience at one of the bloodiest battlegrounds of the Salvadoran civil war and the lives of survivors a quarter-century later.

Innocent Voices (2004) This film tells the story of a boy in El Salvador in the 1980s seeking a normal life while an environment of violence rages around him.

Maria's Story (1991) This documentary tells the story of Maria Serrano, a rural mother and Salvadoran guerrilla leader. At the time the film was made, she was thirty-nine years old and had been in the war for more than ten years.

Index

A

Abrams, Elliot, 142
ADEMUSA (Association of Salvadoran Women), 151
Agrarian reform (El Salvador), 31, 40–41
Agrarian reform (Guatemala), 59, 103
Alas, Jose, 134
Albuquerque Journal (newspaper), 199
Alpirez, Julio Roberto, 159–160
Alvarez, Walter Antonio, 205–207
Alvarez Gómez, Oscar Hugo, 156
Amaya Rosa, Francisco, 204
American Convention on Human Rights, 55
American Declaration of the Rights and Obligations of Man, 89
American Institute for Free Labor Development (AIFLD), 41
Apartheid, 7, 109
Arana Osorio, Carlos, 75
Arbenz Guzmán, Jacobo, 110n3, 159
ARENA (Alianza Republicana Nacionalista/Nationalist Republican Alliance), 36, 130–131, 207
Arévalo, Juan José, 110n3
Argentina, 50
Arnson, Cynthia J., 30–38
Aung San Suu Kyi, 109
Avila, Eduardo Alfonso, 201–202
Axis Rule in Occupied Europe (Lemkin), 5

B

Becklund, Laurie, 199
Benavides, Marta, 187–195
Bolivia, 191
Brockman, James, 203
Buckley, William F., 142
Buried Secrets (Sanford), 66
Bush, George H.W., 47, 78
Byrne, Hugh, 116–124

C

Canada, 191
Carmack, Robert M., 63, 164, 216–227
Carter, Jimmy, 39, 40–42, 203
Castillo Armas, Carlos, 59
Castro, Salvador, 183
Catholic church
closures in Guatemala, 61
priest and nun assassinations (El Salvador), 33, 37, 42, 46–47, 53, 140, 141
priest and nun assassinations (Guatemala), 70, 103
repressive policies, 85
Cave, Damien, 177
Cerezo, Vinicio, 68, 78
Chalk, Frank, 5–14
Chang, Myrna Mack, 69, 79
Chapultepec Agreements, 49–51
Chàvez, Luis, 133–134, 135
Chile, 50
Church workers, 33, 40–41
CIA (US Central Intelligence Agency)
awareness of Guatemalan massacres, 76–77
death of Romero, Oscar, and, 198
funding of El Salvador assassins and, 36